SEND A MESSAGE TO MICKEY

SEND A MESSAGE TO

MICKEY

The abc's of making your voice heard at Disney

Richard D. Land
& Frank D. York

BROADMAN
& HOLMAN
PUBLISHERS

Nashville, Tennessee

©1998 Broadman & Holman Publishers
Nashville, Tennessee
All rights reserved

ISBN 0–8054–9308–5
Printed in the United States of America

Unless otherwise indicated, Scripture quotations are from the *Holy Bible, New International Version* (NIV), copyright ©1973, 1978, 1984 by International Bible Society. Used by permission of Zondervan Bible Publishers.

1 2 3 4 5 6   02 01 00 99 98

If anyone causes one of these little ones who believe in me to sin, it would be better for him to have a large millstone hung around his neck and to be drowned in the depths of the sea. Woe to the world because of the things that cause people to sin! Such things must come, but woe to the man through whom they come!
    — The Lord Jesus Christ, Matthew 18:6–7

Contents

The Disney Boycott: Questions, Answers, and Simple Steps to Success

INTRODUCTION

WHAT WOULD YOU DO?

If you're a parent, imagine taking your family each Sunday after church to an establishment billing itself as a "family restaurant." The restaurant is clean, well lighted, and has a play area for your children. Closed-circuit TVs overhead play cartoons so your children are constantly entertained. The food is great, and your waitress jokes with your children and offers them free ice cream after the meal. There's a feeling of warmth here and you return again and again. In fact, your children beg you to take them there each Sunday—just as they beg you to take them to see Walt Disney movies and buy Disney videotapes and mouse ears.

But what happens to your faith in that restaurant and its friendly waitresses when you discover a back room near the rest rooms, where both children and adults are being exposed to pornographic movies, deviant sexual behaviors, drugs, and alcohol?

Would you lose faith in the management's sincerity when they claim to be family friendly and to love children? Would the back room give you a clear picture of where the management's heart is on the matter? Is this really a family-friendly restaurant, or is the manager just using the front room to fund his back room activities?

Furthermore, would you continue bringing your family each Sunday to this restaurant just because the food is good and the entertainment is wholesome? Would you simply discount what is happening in the back room because it doesn't directly affect you?

Suppose you complained to the manager and all he said to you was, "Well, that's too bad. We're serving good food up front, and we're making millions in the back room." Would you return? Probably not.

By not returning to this restaurant, you are boycotting it. That's what this book is about—your right to determine how you're going to spend your hard-earned dollars on entertainment. You have the right to withhold your dollars from restaurants serving you bad food, and you have the right to withhold spending from organizations that offend your values or harm your children. As you'll see, boycotting is a part of American history. In fact, you probably boycott a product or service much more often than you realize.

POLLUTERS OF THE CULTURE

Our nation has taken a strong stand against environmental pollution. Cities, for example, are not allowed to dump untreated sewage into rivers or lakes. Manufacturing companies also must obey environmental laws. On a more personal level, your neighbor has no right to dump his garbage into your yard every week. Nor do you have the right to run your sewage into the storm drains in your town.

Although most Americans understand the importance of laws protecting us from environmental pollution, there's confusion over the issue of cultural pollution. Yet the cultural pollution we are seeing in our society is far more devastating to our well-being than an occasional oil spill or overturned propane truck on the freeway.

The violent and sexually explicit movies being produced in Hollywood have contributed to a coarsening of our society and a hardening of hearts. Michael Carneal, the teen who killed three high school classmates in Kentucky in December 1997, is a sobering reminder of how cultural pollution can impact our society. News reports indicate that this young man was inspired to kill after seeing a high school murder scene in the movie *The Basketball Diaries*, produced by New Line Pictures. The mind of this teen was polluted by destructive images in a film, and he killed. Several years ago the Time Warner company was taken to task by former Bush administration drug czar William J. Bennett for that company's distribution of violent, obscene rap music. The music glorified killing police officers and raping women. Bennett called on Time Warner to stop distributing antiwoman, antipolice music, and parents were encouraged to boycott Time Warner products to force this entertainment giant to change its policies.

Obscene rap music is one obvious example of cultural pollution, but most parents have been unaware of how The Walt Disney Company has changed over the years. To the casual observer, the Disney public image still brings to mind pleasant thoughts of Mickey Mouse, Snow White, Goofy, and Cinderella. *Yet Disney has changed.* The heart of the Disney management now seems to have more in common with the evil, jealous stepmother in Snow White than it does with the moral purity of the heroine. *Disney has turned to the dark side. And they will continue down this sinister path until they realize responsible parents will not support such a transformation from the unquestioned symbol of family fun to a purveyor of "entertainment" that is offensive to millions.*

BOYCOTTING IN A FREE MARKET

You shop at different places depending on how you're treated and how high the prices are. You usually don't return to a store if you've been insulted repeatedly by the cashiers or the management. You boycott the store and purchase your products elsewhere.

You boycott a car mechanic or used car salesman after being swindled one time—and you will usually warn your friends to stay away from certain dishonest mechanics and salespeople. In effect, you are encouraging a boycott when you warn your friends about a disreputable businessman.

You also boycott when you choose to avoid a restaurant after a particularly bad experience. The health department is supposed to oversee restaurants in a community, but oftentimes adverse publicity in a local paper or on TV can do wonders to change the attitudes of the management and to improve the quality of the food. In the fall of 1997, the CBS affiliate in Los Angeles published on its Web page a listing of the five hundred cleanest and five hundred dirtiest restaurants in the city. The lists were compiled from health department records. If Los Angeles residents carefully read this list, they can choose to boycott the restaurants with bad health department reports and to spend their money at restaurants with good health department records.

In short, you're probably already a boycotter; but this book will provide you with background information on The Walt Disney Company and why you should prayerfully consider withholding your financial support from this media conglomerate.

BOYCOTTING IS AS AMERICAN AS THE AMERICAN REVOLUTION

One of the most colorful and best known events leading up to the American Revolution was a boycott. In 1765 the British passed the Stamp Act, which forced all of the colonists to buy stamps to put on legal papers, magazines, and newspapers. A stamp costing ten dollars was demanded for each college diploma. The colonists rebelled against the Act in a number of ways. Some simply refused to buy the stamps. In Boston, boxes of stamps were seized and burned. The colonists worked to defeat the Stamp Act by refusing to buy British goods, and many of them began to make their own clothing and scorned those who wore linens and woolens imported from England. The boycott injured English trade and brought about unemployment in Britain.

After only four months, the British parliament repealed the Stamp Act. The colonists' victory was short-lived, however. In 1767 Britain passed the Townshend Act, which levied taxes on glass, paper, paints, and tea.

The colonists responded with another boycott, refusing to buy any of these products from England. Many of the colonial businessmen signed nonimportation agreements. They agreed not to stock English products in their stores. In addition, those merchants who did continue carrying British goods found their names listed in the local newspapers. They were soon disgraced and, as a result, lost customers.

THE BOSTON TEA PARTY

The colonists' anger took a more violent turn in December 1773. That month three British tea ships were anchored in Boston's harbor, but they could not be unloaded until the taxes were paid on the cargo. Fearing reprisals from the colonists, the merchants refused to pay the tax.

On the night of December 16, a group of colonists (including John Hancock) dressed up as Indians, boarded the vessels, and threw 342 chests of tea into the harbor. This action intensified the tension between the colonists and Britain. The economic and political conflicts accelerated until all-out war began on Lexington Green on April 19, 1775.

Boycotting was one of the forces that eventually led to the founding of the United States with its freedom of speech, freedom of religion, freedom of conscience, freedom of association, and freedom of the press. We exercise several of those freedoms every time we refuse to purchase a product from The Disney Company.

THE MAGIC KINGDOM HAS BECOME THE TRAGIC KINGDOM

The Walt Disney Company, which has built a worldwide media empire by bringing joy to children, is now producing films that will harm children—films that glorify adultery, incest, violence, and homosexual relationships.

In 1996, in response to the growing nationwide concern over Disney's direction, the Southern Baptist Convention (SBC) passed a resolution urging its 15.7 million members to consider boycotting Disney products. That same year, the Assembly of God denomination urged its 2.5 million members to boycott Disney because the entertainment conglomerate had abandoned the commitment to strong moral values.

If even two million Southern Baptists refrained from spending at least one hundred dollars on Disney products over the next year, that would translate into a two hundred million dollar loss to the Disney Corporation.

The SBC's 1996 Disney Resolution explains why it is important to boycott Disney: "Southern Baptists and their children have for many decades enjoyed and trusted the Disney Co.'s television programming, feature-length films, and theme parks which have reinforced basic American virtues and values. . . . The virtues promoted by Disney have contributed to the development of a generation of Americans who have come to expect and demand high levels of moral and virtuous leadership from the Disney Co., and . . . In recent years, the Disney Co. has given the appearance that the promotion of homosexuality is more important than its historic commitment to traditional family values and has taken a direction which is contrary to its previous commitment."

In June 1997 the SBC meeting in Dallas, Texas, passed a stronger resolution condemning Disney for its production of antifamily, pornographic, and anti-Christian films. The complete text of this resolution is reprinted in Appendix 3.

It is tragic that not only has The Walt Disney Company become aggressive in its apparent promotion of homosexuality; but its publishing companies, its TV network (ABC), and its film production companies appear to be promoting pornography, violence, anti-Christian messages, and New Age spirituality. These are serious issues, and each of them will be explained in detail in later chapters.

Until the mid-1980s, The Walt Disney Company was known around the world for its wholesome family entertainment. The Disney name was one a parent could trust. Disney movies promoted the virtues of honesty, courage, and hard work and were free of profanity, nudity, and graphic violence.

After Walt Disney died in 1966, the company he founded began to experience a slow decline. The visionary was gone, and there seemed to be no one left to maintain Walt's standards of excellence or his commitment to wholesome family entertainment.

In the mid-1980s, Michael Eisner was hired from Paramount Studios to become the new head of The Disney Company. One of Eisner's first acts was to create Touchstone Pictures as a vehicle for producing more adult film fare. One of Touchstone's first films was *Splash*, a film about a mermaid, starring Daryl Hannah and Tom Hanks. Hannah's nudity in a Disney film was a turning point for The Disney Company. In 1986 Touchstone also produced *Down and Out in Beverly Hills*, a story about a homeless man who comes into the lives of a wealthy Beverly Hills couple played by Richard Dreyfuss and Bette Midler. The homeless man, played by Nick Nolte, seduces Midler and their daughter, while Dreyfuss is having an affair with the maid. The adulterous relationships are trivialized as the homeless man wins the hearts of his benefactors.

Eisner's savvy turned Disney around economically but also initiated a moral decline within the entertainment empire that over time has accelerated. As the lure of big dollars has edged out concerns about morality and common decency, Eisner's strategies have worked. Profit and the bottom line seem to be all that matters.

It's ironic that while the Disney empire is still revered by millions of parents around the world who purchase Disney products, attend Disney movies, and watch ABC sitcoms, the values promoted by Disney's subsidiaries are diametrically opposed to the traditional values held by most of them. As a *USA Weekend* public opinion poll conducted in July of 1997 indicated, nearly half of those responding were supportive of a boycott against Disney. A total of 107,000 contacted *USA Weekend* to express their opinions. Of those, 50.5 percent did not support the boycott while 49.5 percent did. *USA Weekend*, a weekly magazine published by the Gannett Company, has more than 41.7 million readers and appears in 496 newspapers across the United States.

It is clear that the boycott is growing, but it will be successful only if parents and concerned citizens understand why Disney is being targeted.

Disney is still producing wholesome entertainment for both adults and children, but now there's a dark side to Disney—a side that is being fed by the dollars of parents who purchase Pooh Bear stuffed animals and Hercules figurines. The dollars parents spend on Mickey Mouse ears and trips to Disneyland and Disney World are helping to fund and energize a company which recognizes homosexual marriages and produces films that normalize anti-Christian values and behaviors.

We have produced this booklet to encourage you to call The Disney Company back to Walt's original vision for his company. It was a vision that supported rather than undermined America's traditional values. As former Disney executive Ken Wales put it not long ago, "When you own a corner on the wholesomeness market, why try something else?" Why indeed.

It's regrettable that "wholesomeness" is not a word that describes The Disney Company in the 1990s. It is no longer a friend of Judeo-Christian values or of children. It is now a captive of anti-Christian philosophies and homosexual activism, and it has become the most aggressive media conglomerate working to normalize deviant sexual behavior. It is truly ironic that the company most closely associated with family-friendly films should now become one of the most hostile enemies of the family and traditional values. Disney has lost its moorings and is trying to have it both ways. As parents realize all that Disney is about, they're going to say: "You can't have it both ways!"

A BOYCOTT WORKS—IN TIME

Donald Wildmon, founder of the American Family Association, has been involved for years in boycotting businesses that sell pornography. "You have to stay with it," says Wildmon. "It's slow to catch on, but once it does, it's about impossible to overcome." Austin Pryor, an AFA supporter and financial planner, agrees with Wildmon's assessment. "To do an effective job of withholding support from objectionable companies, we must be ready to boycott—not their securities [stocks], but their products and services," said Pryor.

"Companies profit from our spending, not our investing. Targeting our routine daily spending can be a potent force for change, as we saw in the recently concluded . . . battle with Kmart over its pornography sales." (AFA was victorious after a five-year boycott of Kmart because its subsidiary company Waldenbooks was selling pornographic books directed to children.)

The key to winning a boycott is to consider it a long-term investment in the future of our culture. Boycotts must be maintained and expanded if they are to work. In addition, those organizations being boycotted must hear from those who are

A British Land Agent Sparks a Rebellion

When Captain Charles Boycott moved to Ireland as a British land agent during the late 1800s, he had no idea that his last name would become synonymous with nonviolent protest.

Boycott was sent to County Mayo, Ireland, as an agent for Lord Erne. His job was to make sure that the lord's crops were harvested before winter. But due to Irish hatred of British landowners, Boycott had to bring in fifty Protestant farm workers, along with a thousand soldiers and police, to protect them as they harvested the crop.

County Mayo's parish priest, Father John O'Malley, organized a protest against what he called the Boycott Relief Expedition. The plan was to initiate a nonviolent protest called "ostracisation" against Boycott. ("Ostracize" would be the modern term.) But O'Malley suggested using the term "boycotting" because it would be easier for his parishioners to pronounce than "ostracisation." Thus "boycotting" entered the English language and is known worldwide as a nonviolent way of protesting economic and social evils.

Boycott was ostracized by the Irish farmers, and the cost of harvesting the crop was astronomical. He eventually returned to England with his family. The anger of the Irish against the English landowners subsided in later years as they were eventually allowed to purchase the land they tilled.

boycotting the products. Although a boycott's effectiveness may eventually be reflected in the company's bottom line, the corporate heads need to know that they're being boycotted—and that they're going to be losing business from formerly loyal customers for a long, long time.

A company stays in business by keeping loyal customers and gaining new ones. If the loyal customers stop buying and new customers are discouraged from purchasing, the company is faced with a dilemma. It must either decide to change its corporate policies to reflect the criticism against it, or ignore the critics and take the losses. With Disney's commitment to the gay agenda apparently firmly in place, it may be unrealistic to expect Michael Eisner to jettison production of pro-homosexual and pornographic movies.

EISNER RESPONDS ON 60 MINUTES

Eisner's assessment of the Christian community's boycott of Disney was clearly revealed in a *60 Minutes* episode on November 23, 1997. His remarks were released to the press earlier in the week. According to Eisner, the boycott "hasn't had a financial effect" on Disney's bottom line, which apparently is all that matters to Disney.

When asked about supporting a gay agenda, Eisner said, "That's ridiculous. We're not pushing any agenda."

Using a broad brush, he also responded to the charges made by many Christians against *Pocahontas*. "When somebody says *Pocahontas* is anti-Christian or anti-Jewish or anti-black or anti-Native American, I say deep down, 'They're nuts. They really are.'" Eisner counters criticism of the historical inaccuracy of the story by saying that Pocahontas' conversion to Christianity didn't occur until after the Disney story ended.

Focus on the Family founder Dr. James Dobson responded to Eisner's printed remarks within days after they were distributed. According to Dobson:

> Unfortunately, *60 Minutes* served up softballs to Michael Eisner regarding the nature of the Disney boycott . . . How does the glorification of brutal violence, homosexuality, drug abuse, and teen sex and the mockery of Christian beliefs reflect Walt Disney's philosophy of family entertainment?
>
> Mr. Eisner's disparaging comments against those who are boycotting Disney as a matter of conscience reveal that he doesn't seem to understand—or care—that families no longer trust Disney. He ridicules those with deeply held religious beliefs who are genuinely concerned about the direction The Disney Company has taken in recent years. He claims that Disney is "not pushing any agenda." We feel that disclaimer is disingenuous....
>
> Mr. Eisner says he is willing to sit down and talk with those participating in the boycott. If that is now true, why has he never made such an offer to this point? I challenge him to live up to this newly proclaimed openness.

So far, Disney has given a deaf ear to our concerns. Its communications department has told our constituents that Disney will not even respond by letter to consumers who send letters of concern on this issue.

I hope that Disney will become more receptive to the views of millions of families who would like Disney to return to the legacy of Walt himself.

Eisner seems to be determined at this point to continue promoting anti-Christian and pro-homosexual materials. In mid-November 1997, ABC announced it was ordering another full season of *Nothing Sacred*. Even though the show's ratings have been low and more than twenty-five sponsors have withdrawn from it, ABC apparently wants to keep it on the air.

Don't you wonder what Walt would have thought? How did the company that gave us the greatest animated film classics in history—the company that was once the unquestioned hallmark of family entertainment—end up in the gutter and decide to stay there?

Boycotts Work!

- The American Family Association boycotted 7-Eleven more than ten years ago because they were the major distributors of pornography in the country through their 4,500 retail stores. After an aggressive two-year boycott, 7-Eleven stopped selling pornography, and other convenience stores stopped as well.
- The Pepsi Cola company sold its 40 percent investment in a local venture in Burma in 1996 because of a boycott against it. Protesters were angry at Pepsi Cola for aiding the economy of a military government that had been accused of terrible human rights violations.
- In 1989 Pepsi Cola also was pressured to pull its TV advertisements featuring Madonna.
- In 1988 the Roy Rogers fast food chain bowed to pressure from the American School Food Services Association for ad campaigns featuring tasteless lunches and mean cafeteria workers in schools.

- In 1989 a group of Christians began boycotting Clorox products because it was advertising on antifamily and indecent TV programs. Within months after the boycott began, Clorox's sales had dropped 12.1 percent. Clorox asked for a meeting with the leaders in Christian Leaders for Responsible Television (CLeaR-TV).
- Several years ago, after an intense boycott by prolife groups, the European pharmaceutical giant Hoechst gave away its rights to the abortion pill, RU-486. Its subsidiary company, Roussel-Uclaf, also distanced itself from the drug. The estimated $3.5 million from sales of RU-486 was not worth risking the $1.63 billion in drug sales in the U.S. Pro-lifers were going to boycott every drug product produced by Hoechst and its affiliates if the company continued to promote the drug.
- International boycotts of South Africa contributed to the overthrow of racial apartheid in that nation.

Chapter 1

Disney's "Tragic Kingdom"

When typical Baby Boomer parents think back about their exposure to Disney's Magic Kingdom, they usually remember Cinderella, Mickey Mouse, or Pooh Bear. But Disney's empire has more recently been characterized as the Tragic Kingdom because of the growing exposure of the dark side of the Disney media giant.

Two events caught the attention of Christian activists and alerted them to a cultural change within the Disney empire. One was the appearance of Gay Days at Disney theme parks each year. Although Disney has denied officially sponsoring these events, it certainly has not done anything to stop them. Unsuspecting parents who have traveled hundreds of miles either to Walt Disney World in Florida or to Disneyland in California have been shocked to see tens of thousands of gays, lesbians, bisexuals, and transvestites flaunting their sexual orientation in front of straight parents and their children.

In 1996, for example, a website promoting Gay Day at Disney World carried a cartoon portraying Mickey Mouse and Donald Duck as homosexual lovers and Minnie Mouse and Daisy Duck as lesbians. Disney was silent about this. Historically, Disney has been careful to protect its image and its properties. For example, Henry Giroux, the Waterbury Chair Professor and Director of the Waterbury Forum for Education and Cultural Studies at Penn State University, pointed out recently that "in its zeal to protect its image and extend its profits, Disney has gone so far as to threaten legal action against three South Florida day-care centers for using Disney cartoon characters on their exterior walls. It's profoundly and sadly ironic that Disney threatens legal action against day-care centers and does nothing to those who co-opt Disney's icons of innocence to promote an event that is so foreign to the spirit of Disney."

The second event that enraged traditionalists was the granting of domestic partner insurance benefits to homosexual lovers. Fifteen Florida legislators were so alarmed at this policy that they wrote a letter of concern to the Disney executives. One of the legislators, a doctor and infectious disease specialist, observed, "I feel this policy is headed in the wrong direction. In the long run, it will result in an increased number of AIDS cases."

The letter continues, "We are surprised at your belittlement of the sanctity of marriage. By implying that vows no longer need to be made in order to gain marital privileges, you are alienating the millions of people in this country who take the marriage covenant seriously and believe that it is ordained by God. We strongly disapprove of your inclusion and endorsement of a lifestyle that is unhealthy, unnatural, and unworthy of special treatment. Those who practice homosexuality are engaging in a lifestyle that should not be given the same status as heterosexual marriages."

When Disney official John Dreyer was asked why domestic partner benefits were not to be extended to heterosexual live-in lovers, he said, "We're just not going to extend it, and we're not really interested in debating it."

Recently Disney contributed money toward the support of a premiere benefit for the Paramount movie *In and Out* starring Kevin Kline and Tom Selleck. The National Gay and Lesbian

Task Force bragged about Disney's support in a press release dated September 8, 1997. One might think it odd that Disney would help throw a party for a competitor's film, but Disney CEO Michael Eisner was formerly the head of Paramount and takes actions and supports policies that will normalize gay lifestyles.

DISNEY'S GAY STAFF

Homosexuals wield enormous power within the "Tragic Kingdom." The May 1995 issue of *Buzz*, a Los Angeles-based magazine, featured an article on Disney entitled "Disney Comes Out of the Closet." The article listed a number of top executives within Disney who are homosexual.

Tom Schumacher, vice president of feature animation, in an interview with Tom Porvenzano of *The Advocate*, said, "I was an out gay man when I came to Disney. I know it is surprising because when people think of this company, they remember gay men not being able to dance together at Disneyland . . . but now there are a lot of gay people here at every level. It is a very supportive environment." Schumacher reported that he has taken his husband on long company retreats. This was offensive to some Disney executives, but not to those who run the company.

In addition to a pervasive homosexual presence within the Disney corporate offices, Disney subsidiaries support homosexual lifestyles. The Disney-owned publishing company Hyperion Press, for example, published *Growing Up Gay*, a book aimed at the gay children of heterosexual parents. The purpose of the book is to normalize homosexual behavior among children. In addition, Hyperion has published *Letting It All Hang Out*, the autobiography of Ru Paul, a black transvestite who has his own half-hour TV talk show on the E! Network. Hyperion also is going to publish a positive book about gay culture and is producing a series entitled *Out and About Gay Travel Guides*, designed to cater to the wealthy gay jetsetters.

Disney has come a long way from its marketing of Pooh Bear storybooks and cuddly Goofy stuffed animals. It is now marketing books aimed at recruiting children into the homosexual lifestyle and which attempt to normalize transvestism.

DISNEY'S SEXUALLY EXPLICIT FILM FARE

Through its subsidiary film companies such as Touchstone Pictures, Hollywood Pictures, and Miramax, Disney is promoting a variety of antisocial themes, including incest. Here's a sampling of the films Disney's film companies have produced during the past several years:

- *Priest* (Miramax). This pro-homosexual movie is also anti-Catholic. It depicts five Catholic priests. One is a homosexual, another is an adulterer, the third is an alcoholic, the fourth is mentally unstable, and the fifth is mean-spirited and vicious.
- *Pulp Fiction* (Miramax). This film was originally rated NC-17 (X) before minimal editing earned it an R rating. It is a seedy, extremely violent movie.
- *Color of Night* (Hollywood Pictures). The director's cut of this movie (available in video stores) features male full frontal nudity and female nudity.
- *Clerks* (Miramax). This movie is about New Jersey convenience store clerks who use such foul language that the film originally earned an NC-17 rating.
- *Kids* (Miramax). According to *Newsweek*, this film "follows a number of barely pubescent looking boys and girls around New York City as they smoke pot, bait gays, beat a black man, and engage in graphic sex." Miramax formed an independent film company to produce this film because of the controversy generated. Perucci Ferraiuolo, writing in *Disney and the Bible*, notes that *Kids* director Larry Clark was interviewed in an issue of *Gayme*, a magazine catering to pedophiles. In the article Clark is shown nude with young boys. Clark's photographic interests allegedly involve teen prostitution, drug use, and suicide.

- **Chicks in White Satin** (Hollywood Pictures). *Chicks* tells the story of a lesbian couple who decide on a semitraditional commitment ceremony.
- *House of Yes* (Miramax). This film is billed as a "comedy" about incest.
- **Sirens** (Miramax). In this film a minister and his wife go to visit an artist who paints portraits of nudes. Three of his subjects are frequently nude in the movie, and one eventually seduces the minister. His wife is seduced by the artist's horse groomer.
- *Trainspotting* (Miramax). The viewer is led on a depressing journey into depravity featuring explicit sex scenes and graphic depictions of intravenous heroin use.
- **The Crying Game** (Miramax). The "hero" in this story is a crossdresser.
- **The English Patient** (Miramax). This Academy Award winning film glamorizes an adulterous affair and promotes euthanasia. The English patient's adultery leads to the betrayed husband crashing his plane into the desert with his wife on board. He dies instantly, and his adulterous wife is seriously injured. The "hero" then collaborates with the Nazis as a means of getting medical help for his lover. She dies in a cave, yet her lover has betrayed the lives of thousands of British and American troops who are fighting the Nazis. The movie ends with a sympathetic approval of active euthanasia as the nurse deliberately kills the badly burned English Patient with an overdose of drugs.

Miramax has long been known for producing raunchy, semipornographic movies, but supporters of the Magic Kingdom may have naively assumed it would clean up its films after it was purchased by Disney. Not so. It seems to be moving more aggressively into sexually explicit and homosexual-theme films. As Miramax President Mark Gill once observed: "Our cheap cliché is sex, betrayal, and murder. You'll see a lot of women with no clothes on their backs in our ads. We'll put a gun in if we can. It works. You can scorn me for this, but it works." Miramax's subsidiary film company, Dimension Films, is building a reputation producing slasher/horror movies such as *Hellraiser III*.

In addition to the films listed above, Disney also produced *Powder*, the story of a young man who has supernatural powers. This dark movie contains overtones of gay sex, but this should not be surprising. The director of the movie, Victor Salva, is a convicted child molester. When critics demanded that Disney fire Salva, Disney's John Dreyer said, "What's the point other than you want to make headlines?"

Disney also has signed Martin Scorcese to a four-year contract. Scorcese is the director of *The Last Temptation of Christ*, a blasphemous film about the crucifixion of Jesus. In this film Jesus is shown as a lunatic who doubted His divinity and was driven by hallucinations and migraine headaches. Scorcese has produced a number of other morally dark films, including *Casino* and *Taxi Driver*.

In 1995 Disney hired Kevin Smith to produce two movies: *Dogma* (scheduled for release in 1998), which asserts that Christian beliefs are little more than mythology; and *Chasing Amy*, about a man who romantically pursues a lesbian. Smith was the screenwriter for *Kids* and *Clerks* as well.

Christians have also criticized Disney for producing *Pocahontas* because it is an inaccurate portrayal of the real-life Pocahontas. Disney scriptwriters rewrote history to create a false portrayal of Pocahontas. The Disney version of Pocahantas shows her as a pagan, earth-worshiping princess who receives wisdom from a tree spirit. She also converts her English boyfriend to a faith in pantheism—the belief that God is a force rather than a personal, caring Creator. Her politically correct extreme environmental views are also evident.

In the historical record of Pocahontas's life she converts to Christianity, marries John Rolfe, a wealthy landowner, and moves to England, where she is treated as royalty. She dies of smallpox before making a return trip to the colonies. Her portrayal in *Pocahontas* is exactly the opposite of what happened in real life. Why do Disney executives feel they have so much freedom to rewrite history for children? And for what purpose other than pushing a radical agenda?

DISNEY BUYS ABC-TV

In 1996 Michael Eisner added a significant piece of real estate to Disney's worldwide communications conglomerate when he purchased Capital Cities/ABC for a reported $19 billion in cash and stock. This is one of the largest corporate mergers in American history, according to a November 10, 1997, Associated Press report. In addition to ABC, Disney also owns Buena Vista Television, Touchstone Television, Caravan Pictures, Walt Disney Television, ESPN, Lifetime, A&E Network, and numerous TV and radio stations throughout the United States.

The Disney Company has started introducing both anti-Christian and pro-homosexual themes in several of its TV shows. As noted earlier, ten out of thirty homosexual characters on TV are on ABC this season, and one can expect that number to increase.

Ellen, of course, has received the most publicity for the coming out of Ellen De Generes, whose real-life lover is Anne Heche. Ellen De Generes' coming out was covered with the same enthusiasm the press showed for covering Princess Diana's life—including a cover story in *Time* magazine. Ellen's producers admitted they hoped this coming out would help teens struggling with their sexual identities to come out as well. As Executive Producer Dava Savel noted, "If this episode helps some child in the Midwest with their sexual identification, we've done our job."

In order to garner as large an audience as possible, Savel recruited Oprah Winfrey, Demi Moore, Laura Dern, k.d. lang, Melissa Ethridge, and Billy Bob Thornton for this episode. Both k.d. lang and Melissa Ethridge are well-known gay activists. Winfrey was chosen to be Ellen's compassionate therapist.

In late April 1998, the future of *Ellen* as a series was in doubt because of ratings.

According to a Gay and Lesbian Alliance Against Defamation (GLAAD) publication on the Internet, ABC will feature homosexual characters on the following shows this season: *Total Security*, Bill Brochtrup, a gay receptionist; *NYPD Blue*, Officer Abby Sullivan; *Spin City*, Carter Heywood, director of minority affairs; *All My Children*, teacher Michael Delaney, student Kevin Sheffield, TV station manager Rudy, and Michael's orthopedic specialist boyfriend, Dr. Brad Phillips; and of course *Ellen*, including Ellen's girlfriend, her friend Peter, and his boyfriend Barrett.

Michael Boatman, the actor who plays Carter Heywood, a gay activist on *Spin City*, was awarded the GLAAD "Outstanding Television Comedy Series" award in 1997 for his positive portrayal of a homosexual. Boatman's character is second in popularity to Michael J. Fox's character on the show. TV networks, with ABC leading the way, are working to introduce other positive gay characters into future programming in order to "normalize" homosexuality.

In addition to pro-homosexual themes in many of ABC's programs, the Disney network began airing *Nothing Sacred* this season. Although a sanitized version of *Priest*, the show depicts the life of Father Ray, a young priest who admits to hating God and who is ambivalent about such things as abortion, promiscuity, and homosexuality. Dozens of organizations have joined in a boycott of advertisers on *Nothing Sacred*, and the boycott seems to have worked. Always a miserable failure in the ratings, *Nothing Sacred* was finally and reluctantly cancelled by ABC.

What is Michael Eisner's response to the Christian concern over the direction he is taking The Walt Disney Company? In an interview in *Business Week* he was asked if the boycott would hurt Disney. "No," he responded. "I'm sorry if the *Ellen* episode in which the lead character declared herself to be a lesbian offends the Baptists. I may not be as religious as some, but I went to a Baptist college [Denison], and I grew up believing that tolerance was the basis of all religions. I think that's missing here—tolerance."

Eisner displays a profound misunderstanding of Baptists and Christianity in general. A *Wall Street Journal* editorial noted that Disney is well aware of why thousands of Americans no longer do business with them. "They have aligned themselves front and center with the homosexual groups who stand diametrically opposed to the Word of Almighty God. Disney is pushing sin, and Christians have no obligation to subsidize it."

Christians may view homosexual behavior as a sin, but homosexual activists are working very hard to portray homosexuality as being benign—akin to being left- or right-handed. In addition, there is a detailed homosexual agenda of which most Americans are unaware. It includes same-sex polygamous marriages and sex with children. And The Disney Company is making it possible for all this to come pouring into your living room.

Chapter 2

Confronting Sins (Even Mickey's)

Have nothing to do with the fruitless deeds of darkness, but rather expose them. For it is shameful even to mention what the disobedient do in secret. But everything exposed by the light becomes visible, for it is light that makes everything visible.

— Ephesians 5:11–14

WE HAVE A DUTY TO CONFRONT SINS

Many Christians are confused about their duty to confront sins – either the sins of a culture or the sins of fellow believers or non-Christian friends. They have grown to assume that the verse "Do not judge, or you will be judged" (Matt. 7:1) means they should never confront another person about his sinful behavior. They also assume this extends to any negative remarks about the sins committed by media giants such as The Walt Disney Company. Yet an honest look at what the Bible says about sin and confrontation shows that we are obligated to confront sin. This is an essential element in our witness for the Lord.

In the October 1997 issue of *SBC Life* (a publication of the Southern Baptist Convention), associate editor John Revell's essay "Confronting the Cultural Darkness" dispels the myths surrounding the idea that we are not to confront sin. As Revell notes:

> The Bible teaches through command and example that God's people, when given the opportunity, have a responsibility to confront the sins of their society. This is not done in lieu of preaching the Gospel, but in tandem with it. Within our own culture, whether the issue is immoral products and practices by a company, or immoral policies by a government, there is ample evidence to support the Christian's responsibility to verbally address those sins and, when appropriate and possible, to take biblically consistent steps to stem the flow of cultural immorality.

The Bible tells story after story of men and women who were called by God to confront the sins of their culture. Confrontation is a theme that is woven throughout the Old and New Testaments.

Prophets such as Elijah, Jeremiah, Ezekiel, Jonah, and others in the Old Testament were called by God to confront sin in their times and to call people to repentance. Their messages were often unpopular, but they were obedient to God even though they suffered persecution as a result of that obedience.

Jeremiah, for example, spent twenty-seven years warning his nation of impending judgment from God because of their sin. He suffered isolation from his family and friends, experienced beatings, and was thrown into a muddy cistern. Yet he continued to faithfully confront the sin in his culture.

In 1 Kings 18:17 the prophet Elijah was called the "troubler of Israel" by King Ahab because he spoke out against the sinful worship of Baal by Ahab, his wife Jezebel, and many of the Jews. He confronted the priests of Baal on Mount Carmel, and the Lord gave him victory. After the Lord brought down fire from heaven to consume the sacrifices of the priests, Elijah took these priests down to the Kishon Valley and had them slaughtered for their pagan idol worship.

Jonah was called by God to preach repentance in the city of Nineveh. After first running away from God, he eventually submitted to the will of the Lord and preached a message of judgment and repentance to the Ninevites. They repented of their sins, and God spared the city from His wrath.

In the New Testament we read the story of John the Baptist and his message of repentance to the nation of Israel. He was so bold in his preaching against sin that he confronted King Herod about his marriage to Herodias, the wife of Herod's brother Philip. Herod had John thrown into prison but was afraid to have him killed because the prophet had such a large following. Herodias, however, conspired with her daughter Salome to have John beheaded. When Salome danced before Herod, he was so pleased with her that he promised to give her anything she desired. When she asked for John the Baptist's head on a platter, Herod had John killed immediately. John's faithfulness to preach against sinful behavior resulted in his death.

As John Revell observes:

> Throughout his ministry, John was notorious for preaching his message of repentance. However, he did not hide himself or his message inside the safety of religious walls. He went out to the peoples of the land. He certainly was not afraid to confront societal sin. . . . These are attempts to influence not merely individuals, but the secular society in which they lived. He called them to turn away from sin and toward God's civil expectations of them. And Jesus affirmed John's actions with high praise, declaring, "Among those born of women there has not risen anyone greater than John the Baptist" (Matt. 11:11).

JESUS CONFRONTED SIN

Jesus always was bold when opposing the religious leaders (the cultural elites) of his day over their sins of hypocrisy and legalism. In Matthew 23 Jesus spoke to a large crowd and openly denounced the Pharisees and the scribes for their sins. In verses 27–28 He pointedly told them: "Woe to you, teachers of the law and Pharisees, you hypocrites! You are like whitewashed tombs, which look beautiful on the outside but on the inside are full of dead men's bones and everything unclean. In the same way, on the outside you appear to people as righteous but on the inside you are full of hypocrisy and wickedness."

Preaching Christ Was Bad for Business

The apostle Paul was certainly not one to avoid confrontation. The Book of Acts and the Pauline Epistles describe in great detail his encounters with the cultural elites of his day. He was stoned, dragged outside the city, and left for dead during one of his encounters with his opponents.

During one visit to Ephesus to preach the gospel, Paul drew the ire of local silversmiths who made a good living making and selling replicas of the goddess Artemis. They conspired to have Paul run out of town.

Why were these businessmen so angry? Because Paul's message was converting pagans to a saving knowledge of Jesus Christ. With more and more men and women turning to Christ, fewer Ephesians were buying silver idols of Artemis. Paul was unintentionally ruining the silversmiths' businesses.

"Paul is not typically identified as a social activist," says John Revell. "Yet, when we consider his pattern, there can be no doubt that he confronted and influenced secular cultures. Wherever he went, he challenged cultural norms that conflicted with God's standards:

"In Lystra he challenged pagan, immoral religion (Acts 14:8–17).

"In Philippi he thwarted a lucrative fortune-telling industry (Acts 16:16–19).

"In Athens he preached against national idolatry (Acts 17:16–34).

"In Ephesus he confronted idol worship and sorcery (Acts 19:9–20, 23–27).

"When he stood before the Roman governor, Felix, Paul challenged him and his wife in matters of righteousness, self-control, and the judgment to come (Acts 24:24–25).

"Granted," continues Revell, "these do not represent Paul's primary goal. His main objective wherever he went was not to merely improve society and see their cultural norms conform to God's standards. It was to proclaim the good news of Jesus Christ and win souls to the kingdom of God's dear Son. Yet, as part of the process, he challenged various sins that were culturally normative. Exposing and confronting the sins of society were essential elements in his evangelism."

The same can be said of the Disney entertainment empire. On the outside parents and children see only Mickey Mouse, the Little Mermaid, and the Magic Kingdom; yet on the inside the Disney empire is full of wickedness and hypocrisy. The Disney Company makes its millions from its wholesome image, and then promotes a pornographic, pro-homosexual, anti-child, anti-Christian agenda with those dollars.

SHOULDN'T WE JUST PRAY AND WITNESS?

Sharing the gospel message is one of the most important elements of what it means to be a Christian, but we are obligated to do more than share our faith verbally. A witness is not only one who verbalizes his faith in Christ. He is someone who acts on his faith by living a life that shows forth what he believes. As Jesus said in Matthew 5:16, "Let your light shine before men, that they may see your good deeds and praise your Father in heaven." In 1 Peter 2:12 we read, "Live such good lives among the pagans that, though they accuse you of doing wrong, they may see your good deeds and glorify God on the day he visits us."

In addition, the Book of James tells us that faith without works is dead. For example, James 2:15–18 says: "Suppose a brother or sister is without clothes and daily food. If one of you says to him, 'Go, I wish you well; keep warm and well fed,' but does nothing about his physical needs, what good is it? In the same way, faith by itself, if it is not accompanied by action, is dead. But someone will say, 'You have faith; I have deeds.' Show me your faith without deeds, and I will show you my faith by what I do."

Throughout the history of the church, the faith of Christians has led them to build hospitals, schools, orphanages, soup kitchens, homes for the poor, and more. They have been motivated to share their faith by doing something for those less fortunate than themselves. Not only have they done good deeds, but they have also had to confront terrible social evils in their cultures.

William Wilberforce, an eighteenth-century British political leader, became a convert to Christianity as a young man. As his understanding of God's calling on his life became more obvious, he wrote in his diary, "Almighty God has set before me two great objectives: The abolition of the slave trade and the reformation of manners."

Wilberforce devoted the rest of his life to abolishing slavery. He helped found several organizations, including the Society for the Education of Africans, the Society for Bettering the Condition of the Poor, and the Society for the Relief of Debtors (which secured the release of fourteen thousand people from debtor's prisons). He also helped establish hospitals for the blind and helped war widows. Wilberforce and others like him who took their Christianity seriously were fulfilling what James described in 1:27: "Religion that God our Father accepts as pure and faultless is this: to look after orphans and widows in their distress and to keep oneself from being polluted by the world."

SAVING THE CHILDREN

Following the spiritual footsteps of Wilberforce, Amy Carmichael, the famous missionary to India, not only preached the gospel to the people of India; she embarked on a lifelong effort to save children from being given or sold into slavery as temple prostitutes. Amy was awakened to the horrors of temple prostitution in 1901 when a seven-year-old girl named Pearleyes managed to escape from one of the temples. In the providence of God, Amy had stopped by to visit the home where this young girl had come for protection.

The temples were places where girls as young as five years of age were brought and "married" to one of the Hindu gods. Many of these girls were actually given to the temple by their parents, thinking it was an honor to have their daughter married to a god.

These unfortunate girls would spend the rest of their lives serving as prostitutes.

To help free and support girls who were involved in temple prostitution, Amy Carmichael founded the Dohnavur Fellowship. By 1923 the Dohnavur Fellowship had thirty homes; and by 1929 more than seven hundred boys, girls, and Christian workers lived in these homes. Because of her work on behalf of these unfortunate children, temple prostitution was eventually banned in India.

As Amy Carmichael looked back on her efforts, she once wrote: "The work was to develop upon lines that would not find general acceptance, and we had to learn the unchangeable truth: our Master has never promised us success. He demands obedience. He expects faithfulness. Results are His concern, not ours. And our reputation is a matter of no consequence at all."

The same can be said for our efforts in boycotting The Walt Disney Company. We have not been promised success, but the Lord values our faithfulness and obedience. The result is up to Him.

In writing about the Disney boycott and the importance of confronting sin, AFA *Journal* news editor Ed Vitagliano says it well: "A boycott places a Christian squarely against something. Whether it was Jonah crying out against a pagan city, Elijah challenging the corrupted people of God, or John the Baptist rebuking a sinful civil leader, the exposing of sin is one of the responsibilities of the Christian. What better way to expose this nation's hedonism and idolatry than to point it out in the policies and practices of a company like Disney, by way of a boycott, and then to issue a call to repentance and faith in the only One worthy of this country's worship—Jesus Christ?"

CONFRONTING IN LOVE

In learning about The Walt Disney Company's production of extremely sexually explicit movies and its promotion of homosexuality, a parent might understandably react in anger. In responding to Disney's antifamily policies, however, the Christian should respond carefully, firmly, and lovingly.

In giving advice to Timothy, the apostle Paul told him in 2 Timothy 2:24–25 that he must not quarrel but should be kind to everyone and willing to teach. In verse 25 Paul said, "Those who oppose him [the Lord's servant] he must gently instruct, in the hope that God will grant them repentance leading them to a knowledge of the truth, and that they will come to their senses and escape from the trap of the devil, who has taken them captive to do his will." That particular verse applies beautifully to any contact a parent may have with The Walt Disney Company. It has certainly been taken captive to do the devil's will.

Proverbs 15:1 also gives wise advice on dealing with opposition: "A gentle answer turns away wrath, but a harsh word stirs up anger." Any message you send to Mickey must be done in love. If the tone of your phone call or letter is hateful, you will only harden the hearts of those on the receiving end of your communication. If hate is generated from your correspondence, let it come from The Disney Company, not from you.

Protect Your Children from Disney's Homosexual Seductions

If the gay agenda is successful in achieving all of its goals, which include abolishing the age of sexual consent for children, what part will Michael Eisner have had in helping to transform the seduction of children into a life-threatening lifestyle? What role, for example, did Eisner play in having Ellen DeGeneres appear on *Sesame Street* and *Storytime* on PBS in early November 1997?

Will children who are seduced into a homosexual lifestyle by Disney's films and sitcoms become like those in India's temple? What will happen to children who are seduced into homosexuality because it was normalized by The Disney Company? How many boys and girls will die of HIV-related diseases because they were taught by Disney that homosexual behavior is normal and good? You may wish to ask these questions of Mr. Eisner.

Chapter 3

Who's Involved in the Disney Boycott?

More than a dozen profamily groups are supporting a boycott of The Walt Disney Company. Several of the more visible groups are the Southern Baptist Convention, Catholic League for Religious and Civil Rights, American Family Association, Concerned Women for America, Focus on the Family, Assemblies of God, PCA, Church of God (Cleveland, Tenn.), and the D.C.-based Family Research Council.

The **American Family Association** is certainly the most experienced in conducting boycotts. Methodist minister Donald Wildmon founded AFA in the early 1980s and has launched dozens of boycotts against such business giants as Kmart, Clorox, Burger King, and Time Warner. Several years ago AFA encouraged a boycott of ABC—before it was owned by Disney—for its sexually explicit TV series *NYPD Blue* produced by Steve Bochco. Bochco takes pride in pushing the envelope on sexual content and profanity in his series. According to the *American Family Journal*, published by AFA, the network lost millions in advertising revenue over *NYPD Blue* but was willing to keep it on the air. In this case, ideology won over the bottom line, and the show is still being broadcast on Disney's watch.

AFA has specialized in targeting advertisers who run ads on morally questionable programming and against such convenience stores as 7-Eleven, which once carried pornographic magazines. After a two-year educational battle against 7-Eleven (which included picketing), the company's corporate headquarters gave in to the pressure and pulled the magazines.

AFA launched its boycott of The Disney Company two years ago, and since then other groups have come on board. Access AFA's Internet Web site (http://www.afa.net/index) for updates on the boycott. You can also download a detailed discussion of the homosexual agenda, "Homosexuality in America: Exposing the Myths," from AFA's Web page.

The New York-based **Catholic League for Religious and Civil Rights,** headed by William Donohue, launched its boycott against Disney in March 1995 after learning that Disney subsidiary Miramax was releasing *Priest,* one of the most anti-Christian and pro-homosexual movies ever produced.

In a press released dated March 28, 1995, Donohue noted: "We are calling for a boycott of all Disney products, a boycott of vacations to Disney World and Disneyland, and a boycott of the Disney cable television channel. We are also asking the public to call Disney and tie up the lines by making a complaint. This is not something that might happen; rather it is something that is already underway. Indeed, Disney has already disabled one of its phone numbers due to the public's response."

Donohue also said the Catholic League was going to take out full-page ads against Disney and would ask all Catholic groups to sell whatever stock they might have in Disney. In September 1996 the Archdiocese of Oklahoma City divested itself of all Disney stock as a protest against the entertainment giant.

The Catholic League has increased its aggressive boycott against Disney since ABC launched *Nothing Sacred,* an antireligious drama about a young priest who doubts his faith, is pro-homosexual, and is confused about abortion.

According to Donohue, *Nothing Sacred* is "nothing more than a political statement against the Catholic Church. The goal is to put a positive spin on Catholic priests who prefer Hollywood's libertine vision of sexuality to the moral teachings of the Church. This propaganda is fodder for dissenting Catholics and anti-Catholic bigots alike. We hope that others will join with us in what is only the beginning of our protest."

Since the boycott of *Nothing Sacred* advertisers began, more than thirty advertisers have pulled out. The Catholic League maintains a Web site to keep its members informed on the progress of the boycott against ABC.

The **Southern Baptist Convention** has also taken a leading role in boycotting Disney, not only for *Nothing Sacred* but for its pro-homosexual and sexually explicit movies. The SBC's Ethics & Religious Liberty Commission (ERLC) maintains an active Web site (www.erlc.com) with regular updates on its efforts. The ERLC, for example, has produced Disney fact sheets, bulletin inserts, and commitment cards, which can be downloaded from the Internet or ordered in bulk. The ERLC is maintaining this site for families who want to stay abreast of the scriptural perspective on cultural issues. The ERLC has also produced a thirty-minute video, *The Disney Boycott: A Just Cause*, designed to be shown in churches. It can be ordered from The Ethics and Religious Liberty Commission.

Tom Elliff, president of the Southern Baptist Convention (1996–1998), has observed: "In recent years the Walt Disney Corporation . . . with a corporate umbrella which includes Touchstone, Miramax, Hollywood Pictures, and Hyperion Press . . . began producing material of graphic violent and sexual content (including total frontal nudity). Additionally, corporate leaders have determined to push an agenda through its productions which portrays anything but the biblical standards for the family in the areas of morality, sexuality, and fidelity. . . . The issue is not bringing Disney down. The issue is whether Southern Baptists will be catalysts for a spiritual awakening by rising up to the standards of God."

The ERLC's Web site provides more details about the Disney boycott as well as a sample letter. For more details about the work of the Ethics and Religious Liberty Commission, write: ERLC, 901 Commerce, Suite 550, Nashville, TN 37203.

The **Family Research Council** has joined the boycott as well. FRC maintains a Web site (http://www.frc.org/html) that deals with a variety of profamily concerns. It has a number of excellent studies and position papers explaining the gay rights movement and the homosexual attack on the family and children. These articles are downloadable for distribution in churches. Parents may wish to download " 'Homosexual Correctness' Advances in America's Schools" by Peter LaBarbera. This paper details how children and teens are being targeted with the message, "Gay is okay." FRC probably produces more research on the gay rights movement than any other profamily group in the United States.

Focus on the Family's Dr. James Dobson is supporting the boycott through radio broadcasts, informative articles in *Citizen* magazine, a fact sheet, "Citizen Issues Alert" (a weekly fax newsletter), and regular updates on *Family News in Focus*, the public policy radio program. On August 27, 1997, Dr. Dobson went on the air to urge millions of Focus listeners to join the boycott against Disney. Dobson said Focus will promote the slogan "Families Can't Trust Disney."

"There's a motive behind this" kind of programming on ABC, he said. "We're talking about an agenda of a movement, and we must oppose it because it is anti-Christian from top to bottom." For regular updates on Focus's involvement, access its Web site and read downloadable news reports from *Family News in Focus*.

Concerned Women for America, founded by Beverly LaHaye, joined the boycott of Disney in 1997. CWA's position on Disney was detailed in "The Tragic Kingdom's Fall from Grace," published on the Internet. "Disney," notes the author, "is an integral part of our history, our culture, and our heritage. It would be a pity to allow Mickey Mouse to become the poster child for the homosexual movement. It also would be sad if we could no longer freely bring our children to the Disney theme park, or to Disney movies, because executives insist on kowtowing to a small minority of people who do not represent America. It is time for American families to speak out. We must let Disney know that we expect better."

The Information Site for the Disney Boycott is not an organization but an Internet site maintained by Jerry Nixon, an activist based in Missouri. Nixon's Web site (http://falcon.laker.net/webpage/boycott.htm) probably is the most extensive news source currently available on the boycott.

These organizations can provide everything you need to stay informed on the boycott and to be effective in letting your voice be heard. These groups are providing you with free information via the Internet. Support them with your donations; they're working on your behalf!

Organizations Boycotting Disney

American Family Association
American Life League
Americans United for the Pope
Ancient Order of Hiberians
Association of Independent
  Methodists
Cardinal Mindszenty Foundation
Cardinal Newman Foundation
Catholic League for Religious
  and Civil Rights
Catholic Answers, Inc.
Catholic Coalition of
  Westchester
Catholic Defense League of
  Minnesota
Chinese Catholic Information
  Center
Church of God (Cleveland,
  Tenn.)
Church of the Nazarene
Citizens for a Better America
Concerned Women for America
Congregational Holiness Church
Coral Ridge Ministries

Family Research Council
Focus on the Family
Free Will Baptists
General Assembly of Regular
  Baptists
International Church of the
  Foursquare Gospel
League of Catholic Voters
Legatus
Jewish Action Alliance
Jews for Morality
King for America, founded by
  Alveda King, niece of Dr.
  Martin Luther King, Jr.
Morality in Media
Muslim Coalition/Peace Press
  Association
Presbyterian Church in America
Pro-Life Action League
Sons of Italy, Commission for
  Social Justice
Southern Baptist Convention
Women for Faith and Family

Chapter 4

Answers to Objections about Boycotting

If you decide to join the Disney boycott and become aggressive about it, you'll soon find a number of people telling you that you're wasting your time. They'll tell you not to expect nonbelievers to act like Christians and that you should be praying or witnessing more. Others will tell you that you'll turn people away from Christ by boycotting Disney. And you'll find others saying that you should only boycott the bad and support the good that Disney does.

In this chapter we'll examine some of those objections and provide you with some solid responses to them.

OBJECTION:
BOYCOTTS DON'T WORK.

Fact: Boycotts do work. But they take time and determination. It can take from five to ten years for a boycott to have its intended effect, according to Todd Putnam, editor of the *National Boycott News*. There are seldom quick victories because the corporation being boycotted figures that its unhappy customers will eventually just give up and start buying their products again. Commitment and persistence are the keys to victory. Refer to this book's introduction for several examples of successful boycotts.

OBJECTION:
WE SHOULD SUPPORT THE GOOD AND BOYCOTT THE BAD.

Fact: If a "family-friendly" restaurant is serving good food to you and your family but is also showing pornographic movies to children in the back room, do you continue visiting the restaurant? Do you "boycott" the back room while still giving money to the restaurant so it can continue to fund its back room activities? By supporting Disney's good films, you're also helping fund Miramax's movies promoting homosexuality, incest, and pornography. Every dime you give to Disney helps fuel its aggressive pro-homosexual agenda.

OBJECTION:
WE SHOULD BUY DISNEY STOCK SO WE CAN CONTROL IT.

Fact: Those who already own stock in Disney will begin to exert their influence on the company if it begins to lose money because of the boycott. Driven by a concern for their profits, they will push the company toward more wholesome entertainment and profamily policies if they find they're going to lose millions of dollars because of your efforts.

OBJECTION:
THE BOYCOTT IS TOO BROAD. WE CAN NEVER WIN.

Fact: You can be as broad or as specific as you want to be in your own personal Disney boycott effort. You can let Disney know you're going to withhold spending for the next ten years if it takes that long to send a message to Mickey.

Make out a list of all of the things you were going to purchase from Disney and send the list to Michael Eisner. If the Disney Channel is part of your basic cable service, have the cable company block it. Under the Cable Act of 1984, cable companies are required to block a station if you request it. And tell Eisner you've had it blocked. If the Disney Channel begins losing millions of viewers, advertisers may be forced to shift their marketing dollars to other networks. Boycott Disney.com on the Internet and tell Eisner about it!

If you have a Disney Store in your town, write a letter to the manager and tell him you're not going to shop there as long as Disney is promoting a pro-homosexual agenda.

OBJECTION:
WE CAN'T DENY OUR KIDS THE ENJOYMENT OF GREAT DISNEY MOVIES.

Fact: There are plenty of wholesome alternatives to Disney films. Available from Baptist Book Stores and Lifeway Christian Stores are *Secret Adventures* and *Veggie Tales* (call 800-233-1123). Or check your local Christian bookstore for ideas. Focus on the Family is a leading producer of quality programming for kids, including *Adventures in Odyssey* and *McGee and Me*. Check out Focus on the Family's Web site for details.

Other film companies produce family-friendly movies and cartoons. Check the movie section of your newspaper or movie databases on the Internet for details. Use key words such as "family friendly" on your Internet search.

OBJECTION:
WE SHOULD JUST PRAY
FOR THE DISNEY EXECUTIVES.

Fact: When you get up in the morning, you don't just pray about eating, do you? You probably sit down and eat breakfast. You don't just pray about going to work either. You get up and go. Your prayers should be linked to action. Yes, pray for the Disney executives, but take action too. Concerned Women for America's slogan is "Prayer and Action." That's good advice for all of us.

OBJECTION:
WE'RE GOING TO CAUSE FINANCIAL
HARDSHIP TO THE GOOD PEOPLE EMPLOYED
BY DISNEY.

Fact: When you purchase a Ford from a local dealership, are you concerned about causing financial hardship among the employees at the local Chrysler dealer? What about the Honda salesmen? Do you worry about the employees at Safeway when you prefer to shop at Piggly Wiggly or Kroger? The truth is, if enough people in town prefer Safeway, the competing grocery may eventually go out of business. People may lose their jobs, but this occurs in a free market society. Are you responsible? Or is this simply a matter of people making free choices in an open society about what is best for themselves and their families?

In addition, many Disney employees have confidentially expressed support for the boycott and its aim to return Disney to the family-friendly policies of its founder.

A good company will keep its customers and gain new ones. A company that cheats its customers or gives them an inferior product will eventually shut down. Back to the analogy of the restaurant with pornography in the back room: Wouldn't it be better for that restaurant to shut down and the good waiters and waitresses to get other jobs, than for the restaurant to stay in business and destroy children in the back room? Perhaps a financial downturn would be healthy for Disney.

OBJECTION:
A BOYCOTT ISN'T CHRISTIAN.

Fact: Is it more Christian to give your money to an organization that is anti-Christian? The American Family Association published an excellent article on this topic, and it's posted on the Internet (http://www.afa.net/index). The issue, says AFA, is one of stewardship and holiness. "The Lord Jesus characterized His followers as stewards, or managers, of all that He gives them, calling them to dispense these resources—including their money—on His behalf and in a responsible manner." How are you spending the money the Lord has given you? Are you spending it on things that please Him or that bring shame to His name?

AFA Journal news editor Ed Vitagliano notes: "Christian responsibility in a fallen world and in an often hostile culture is expressed by at least two well-known New Testament symbols: The believer is called to be the salt of the earth and the light of the world (Matt. 5:13–16). The follower of Christ is a light in a darkened world first by the preaching of the gospel (2 Cor. 4:4–6) and second by the good works which the believer performs (Matt. 5:16). In these two ways, God's truth is manifest by both word and deed to point unbelievers to the Savior.

"Salt represents a preserving quality of Christians. In society, the Lord's disciples are to resist the corruption of the world and to add blessing to it. When Christians cease this function, Jesus said they have lost their flavor and have become worthless to the work of the kingdom. This saltiness of the Christian is first evidenced by his refusal to live according to the sinful ways of the world. Paul said, 'Do not participate in the unfruitful deeds of darkness' (Eph. 5:11). 'In this sense, the SBC [Southern Baptist Convention] boycott of Disney is certainly legitimate,' said Charlie Reese, a columnist for *The Orlando Sentinel.* 'The Baptists are seceding from decadence,' he said."

OBJECTION:
BOYCOTTING IS CENSORSHIP.

Fact: Censorship is rightly defined as the act of a government entity restraining a media outlet from publishing or broadcasting something. Boycotting is the nonviolent choice of a person to refuse to spend his money at a particular business. It has been likened to high-visibility counteradvertising. While the businessman is free to advertise his products, the boycotter is free to advertise his refusal to buy those products. That's the beauty of the American system of free enterprise and free speech.

OBJECTION:
BOYCOTTING HARMS OUR WITNESS.

Fact: The boycott of Disney has allowed Christians to explain many times to society, through multiple media outlets, God's standard of righteousness and to give a biblical witness against pagan sexuality and homosexuality.

At last count, the Disney boycott has given me twenty-seven specific new opportunities to explain the gospel through the media and to people I would not otherwise have had access or opportunity to do so.

Chapter 5

Send a Message to Mickey

You can send a message to Mickey in a number of ways. The first thing you can do is to begin boycotting Disney products and services. But boycotting is only half of the equation. Disney needs to know you're boycotting.

Write a letter to express your concern about and disappointment in Disney. The Southern Baptists' Ethics and Religious Liberty Commission has provided its supporters with a sample letter to stimulate your thinking. We are reprinting the letter here, but do not copy it verbatim. Letters that appear copied or "canned" carry much less influence at the corporate level than letters obviously written from individuals. The letter you write should reflect your expressions of disappointment that you can no longer purchase Disney products or attend Disney theme parks. Study the example and use ideas from it in your own correspondence:

SAMPLE LETTER TO DISNEY CEO
MICHAEL EISNER FROM CWA MEMBERS

Chairman Michael Eisner
The Walt Disney Company
500 South Buena Vista Street
Burbank, California 91521

Dear Chairman Eisner:

We agree with and are participating in the growing financial protest against your corporation and its entities to express our displeasure with your current policies and direction. We believe these policies are in direct opposition to the moral standards that we, as Christians, hold to be absolute. As a result of your company's radical shift away from a wholesome, pro-family philosophy, my family did not spend the following amount on your products this month:

Movies: _____

Videos: _____

Merchandise: _____

Theme Parks: _____

Other: _____

We continue to pray that you will return to the corporate and pro-family policies of your corporation's founder, Mr. Walt Disney.

Sincerely,

cc: The Ethics & Religious Liberty Commission

901 Commerce, Suite 550

Nashville, Tennessee 37203

DISNEY BOYCOTT WEB SITE

Jerry Nixon, a Christian activist based in Missouri, has set up an information site on the Internet to keep Disney boycotters informed on the progress of the boycott. He provides his readers with the following sample letter to Michael Eisner:

The Walt Disney Company
Chairman Michael Eisner
500 S. Buena Vista Street
Burbank, CA 91521
August 25, 1997

Dear Mr. Eisner:

As I am sure you know, the Christian community has begun to move against the Disney Corporation. Please know that the boycott initiated by the American Family Association and then the Southern Baptists during the summer convention in 1997 is not something that is enjoyable—for either group, including Disney.

I am a Christian. I have watched Disney change as years have passed. I have hoped in my heart that these changes in Disney productions—New Age sentiments and questionable content—would stop and return to the clean and wholesome entertainment I could trust with my children.

Now, I have learned that the Disney internal policies are the same as their new outward productions. In following the crowd, you have begun to create an environment that supports an alternative lifestyle which I feel is counterproductive to the family, not just my family but the family that up until recently I never doubted that Disney advocated.

I know we are in agreement. Your web site FAMILY.COM says nothing about homosexuality or same-sex families. When you say "family," it appears we do indeed mean the same thing. I support the family and am writing you because I want to remind you that you too support families, or at least you used to. I used to trust my children with you. I used to look forward to your next release or new book or our trips to Disney World.

Things have changed, though, haven't they? Subsidiaries of Disney are hiring child molesters to direct movies. Some publish books that advocate homosexuality and encourage children to foster gay tendencies. Miramax produces movies with content so horrible that the NC-17 rating had to be used—and I feel and know I am responsible.

I have sat quietly for a long time watching. I have continued to see your movies, attend your theme parks, wear your clothes, and rent your videos. I have funded it too long, far too long. The actions The Disney Company is taking are wrong. I do not and will not agree with the influence you are exercising over me, my children, and the rest of society as the largest player in the entertainment industry.

Perhaps one person does not matter to you. Perhaps getting a letter from me will not change your course of action. But, personally, I have to stop somewhere. The Disney boycott has awakened my conscience. I am joining the Disney boycott. No more movies. No more clothes. No more videos. No more theme parks. No more cartoons. No more Disney Channel. No more *Disney* magazine. No more Disney World, or MGM Theaters, or Epcot Center or Disneyland. No stuffed animals, computer mouse pads, screen savers, pencils, watches, mouse-eared hats. None. Nothing more.

Until the Disney Corporation begins to visibly show a change in its direction. Until the Disney Corporation clearly becomes trustworthy again with my children. Until Disney or subsidiary films don't have the NC-17 rating. Until Disney or subsidiary publishers are no longer advocating homosexuality. And until internal employee policies again reflect the family values Walt Disney helped glorify when he was alive. Until then my family and all those I influence will boycott the Walt Disney Corporation completely.

I do not make this claim lightly. It is in no way a threat but a plea. I cannot wait until I can enjoy Disney creations again. I hope you take me seriously and the message sent out by the Christian community through the American Family Association and the Southern Baptists. This is no small matter.

I don't know what decisions you face, and I am sure they are difficult. But I do know you matter to God. I know you have the ability to change lives with the influence of your company. I know you have been given much, and because of that you can give much. I will pray for you and your family, and that you will have the wisdom and then the strength to do what is right.

Sincerely yours,

WHAT ELSE CAN YOU DO?

In addition to writing letters to the corporate headquarters of Disney, you can also write to the subsidiaries to let them know you will not be purchasing their products or attending their movies. If you have Internet access, you'll find that many of these corporations have their own Web sites and E-mail addresses. Search the Internet for Disney's subsidiaries and begin E-mailing your concerns to them. E-mailing is becoming one of the most efficient ways of communicating with others. You can set up an E-mail mailing list of Disney subsidiaries and send one letter to dozens of them in the time it would take to write out and send a letter through the mail. You can also ask for a return receipt so you'll know which E-mails went through. There is no guarantee you'll receive an answer, but you can be sure corporate executives will be counting the E-mails they receive.

HERE'S A LIST OF OTHER THINGS YOU CAN DO TO BOYCOTT DISNEY:

1. Write a letter to every theater manager in your town, letting them know you will be boycotting any films produced by The Walt Disney Company or its subsidiaries.

2. Write a letter to the managers of the video stores in your community and tell them you will not be renting any videos produced by Disney or its subsidiaries. Explain why.

3. If you have a Disney Store in your community, let the manager know you will not shop in his store. Make sure you let him know it's not personal but that you cannot buy products from a company that is producing pornography and promoting a gay agenda.

4. Access Disney.com on the Internet and send an E-mail message to Disney executives telling them of your intent to boycott.

5. If you have received a Disney product catalog in the mail recently, return the catalog to them with a letter explaining why you will not purchase anything from Disney. Write The Disney Catalog, Inc., at 5780 Challenge Drive, Memphis, TN 38115.

6. If you receive promotional material from Disney World or Disneyland, send the materials back with a letter explaining why you will no longer take your family to Disney-owned theme parks.

7. Contact ABC and tell them you will no longer watch their network as long as they are airing shows such as *Ellen* or *Nothing Sacred*, a series that denigrates religious faith. ABC's executives can be reached by writing ABC Standards & Practices, 24 East 51st St., New York, NY 10022-6887; or call 212-456-7777.

8. If The Disney Channel is a premium channel in your area, contact your local cable station and ask that it be removed from your service.

9. Disney owns a cruise line, travel service, and vacation clubs. Whenever you receive promotional literature from them, return it with a letter describing why you're boycotting.

10. If you subscribe to any of the magazines owned by Disney (and listed in Appendix 4), consider canceling your subscription and telling them why.

11. If you live in the Los Angeles area, you can boycott the Anaheim Angels and the Mighty Ducks Hockey team—both owned by Disney.

12. Write or E-mail a letter to the editor of your local newspaper about the boycott.

13. Join or support with your prayers the numerous organizations involved in the boycott. These organizations need your help. The largest and most influential of these groups are:

Southern Baptist Convention, 901 Commerce, Suite 750, Nashville, TN 37203, 615-244-2495 (and the Convention's Ethics and Religious Liberty Commission, 901 Commerce, Suite 550, Nashville, TN 37203, 615-244-2495)

American Family Association, P.O. Drawer 2440, Tupelo, MS 38803, 800-326-4543, 202-488-7000

Focus on the Family, Colorado Springs, CO 80995, 800-232-6459

Catholic League for Religious and Civil Rights, 1011 First Ave., New York, NY 10022, 212-371-3191

Concerned Women for America, 901 D Street, SW, Suite 800, Washington, D.C. 20024, 202-488-7000

Family Research Council, 801 G Street, NW, Washington, D.C. 20001, 800-225-4008

Each of these organizations has an Internet site so you can keep instantly updated on the status of the boycott.

14. Support organizations involved in ministering to or providing therapy for homosexuals. Contact Exodus International at P.O. Box 77652, Seattle, WA 98177-0652, 206-784-7799; and the National Association for the Research and Therapy of Homosexuality at: NARTH, 16542 Ventura Blvd., Suite 416, Encino, CA 91436; 818-789-4440; E-mail: info@narth.com.

15. Start buying children's videos from profamily resources. Focus on the Family has a variety of videos and books for children. You may wish to contact Eden Communications, a ministry of Films for Christ for a catalog of wholesome family films. You can access their Internet site or write Eden Communications, 1044 N. Gilbert Road, Gilbert, AZ 85234; 800-332-2261; FaithWorks, founded by John Schneider, costar of the TV series *Dukes of Hazzard,* is producing a number of family-friendly films, including a three-part documentary entitled *Whatever Happened to America?* narrated by Schneider. For more information on FaithWorks call 888-692-9124 or E-mail a request for information to tpfromla@aol.com. FaithWorks also has an Internet site.

16. Start a small newsletter in your church to keep the pastor and church members informed about the boycott and Disney's activities.

17. Join together with friends to pray that Michael Eisner's heart will be softened and that he will bring Disney back to the purpose and practices that has had a wholesome influence across the world. Pray for Eisner's salvation and for a spiritual revival to come to Disney. Pray also that Disney will stop promoting immorality in its films and videos. To contact Michael Eisner write The Walt Disney Company, 500 South Buena Vista Street, Burbank, CA 91512; or call 818-560-1000.

In short, do what you feel called to do to bring Disney back to its historic tradition of providing families with wholesome, positive, and morally uplifting films. If this booklet has helped motivate you to do something, it will have served its purpose. May the Lord bless your efforts.

How <u>You</u> Can Make the Disney Boycott a Success

1. Boycotting a Disney product will do no good if The Disney Company is unaware that you're boycotting. You must let the company know. The easiest way to inform Disney of your boycotting efforts is to write a letter to them. If you are on-line and know how to get around on the Internet, you can E-mail them your concern through Disney.com.

2. Let Disney know exactly why you are boycotting, how many people are in your family, and how many people in your church are going to be boycotting.

3. Tell Disney what you are going to boycott. Do not give Disney any indication when you might stop boycotting. You may wish to boycott every product that comes out of Disney as well as its TV programs and films.

4. Ask Disney officials if they truly understand what the gay agenda is trying to accomplish and quote sections of Appendix 2 from *Send a Message to Mickey* about the gay agenda. Recommend to Disney officials some of the groups, publications, and ministries mentioned at the end of this book. They may ignore the information you give them, but they will be responsible for the knowledge they have been given.

5. Don't destroy Disney items you already own. It will be confusing enough for your young children to understand why your family will no longer purchase Disney materials. You will cause even more distress if you tear up your child's Pooh Bear or throw away those Mickey Mouse sheets.

---

6. Stay informed on this issue. The Internet is one of the best ways to keep up to date on the progress of the Disney boycott. You may also wish to subscribe to magazines or donate to organizations involved in the boycott. These groups have taken a principled stand. They should be supported with your dollars and your prayers. If you're connected to the Internet, you can stay informed by accessing the Web sites of: The Ethics and Religious Liberty Commission of the Southern Baptist Convention; the American Family Association; Focus on the Family; Christian Coalition; Concerned Women for America; and The Information Site for the Disney Boycott. In addition, Exodus International, a ministry to homosexuals, maintains a wealth of information on its Web site, as does the National Association for the Research and Therapy of Homosexuals (NARTH). You can also subscribe to *Light,* an ethics news journal, published by the Ethics & Religious Liberty Commission; *Citizen* magazine, published by Focus on the Family; CWA's journal; the *AFA Journal*; *Christian American*, published by the Christian Coalition; and *SBC Life*, published by the Southern Baptist Convention. Addresses for these groups are provided elsewhere in this book.

7. Pray that Michael Eisner and his chief executives will experience a genuine change of heart over the promotion of homosexuality, adultery, incest, New Age ideas, and pornographic movies.

8. Don't wear yourself out. Pace yourself and realize that a boycott victory against Disney may take five years or longer. It took William Wilberforce more than twenty years to achieve the abolition of the slave trade in England.

Appendix 1: The Power of the Media

WHO'S IN CHARGE HERE?

The media spend hundreds of millions of dollars each year to influence our buying decisions. How many times have you ordered pizza on a Friday night after seeing an advertisement on TV for a special deal at the local Pizza Hut or Little Caesar's? Or seen a movie because of a clever ad campaign? To deny that the media can influence us is to fly in the face of reality. The media exists to influence us—for better or ill.

The media elite in Hollywood understand the power they have to influence us, not only to purchase cars and pizza but to influence our attitudes and values as well. Although they seldom state this publicly, there are times when a few of them are candid about the power they wield.

In November of 1991, George Lucas spoke at a ground-breaking ceremony at a new facility at the USC Film and Television School. Lucas noted:

Film and visual entertainment are a pervasively important part of our culture, an extremely significant influence on the way our society operates. . . .

People in the film industry don't want to accept the responsibility that they had a hand in the way the world is loused up. But, for better or worse . . . films and television tell us the way we conduct our lives, what is right and wrong. It's important that the people who make films have ethics classes, philosophy classes, history classes. Otherwise, we're witch doctors.

THE WITCH DOCTORS

Writing in *What Is Secular Humanism?* historian James Hitchcock devotes a chapter to the power of the mass media to influence our attitudes and behaviors. He notes that the de-Christianization of the mass media began to take place in the mid-1960s, with the most dramatic changes taking place in the 1970s.

Hitchcock observes that prior to the 1960s, the mass media generally supported what has been called traditional values, or the Judeo-Christian ethic in American culture. "In the past," notes Hitchcock, "whatever youth culture existed—literature for young people, for example, or Walt Disney films—aimed to integrate youth into the values of the adult world. There was no contradiction between the content of the youth media and the beliefs of parents. . . . Now, however, the youth culture is explicitly opposed to parental values, sets itself up as a rival authority, and seeks to prolong adolescent attitudes throughout life."

Hitchcock says it was Norman Lear who led this effort to secularize the mass media. It was Lear's belief that entertainment should be used to change the attitudes of middle-class America to support liberal social agendas and causes. Lear's successful series *All in the Family* portrayed Archie Bunker as a mindless, bigoted American whose views had to be changed by his enlightened liberal son-in-law, played by Rob Reiner.

As Hitchcock notes, "People accepted ideas in the guise of entertainment which they would have rejected indignantly had they been confronted with them outright."

In 1980 Norman Lear founded People for the American Way, an organization that has worked incessantly to strip our nation of any semblance of a Christian heritage. More recently, Lear has joined the board of trustees of Hollywood Supports, a group dedicated to the introduction of pro-homosexual themes in movies and TV. Disney chairman Michael Eisner is also a trustee of Hollywood Supports.

THE POWER OF THE MESSAGE

Hollywood has recently taken a stand against smoking and is working to reduce the incidences of smoking in its TV programming and in movies. It has also agreed, in principle, to reduce its glorification of drug use. Yet sexual promiscuity, extreme violence, and nudity are not yet considered taboos among the Hollywood elite. While it's all right to portray explicit sexual activities on the screen, it's not politically correct to light up a cigarette after such an encounter.

Hollywood is conveying powerful messages and images in its films and TV programs. Are the messages of sexual promiscuity and violence having an impact on our culture? Current research and contemporary real-life examples would certainly say so.

In *Don't Touch That Dial—The Impact of the Media on Children and the Family*, authors Barbara Hattemer and Robert Showers provide the reader with convincing evidence that Hollywood's negative messages are provoking children and teens to violent acts and premarital sexual activity. These messages are also helping youth form attitudes toward sexual behavior. Hattemer and Showers discuss a study done of seventh- and ninth-grade students in Rhode Island on how their attitudes were affected by media messages promoting premarital sex. Of seventeen hundred children studied, 65 percent of the boys and 47 percent of the girls agreed it was "acceptable for a man to force sex with a woman if he had been dating her for more than six months." One quarter of the boys and one-sixth of the girls said it was "acceptable for a man to force a woman to have sex if he has spent money on her."

Is the entertainment industry also responsible, in part, for encouraging violent behavior in children and teens? A study conducted by Drs. Eron and Huesmann followed eight-year-olds for twenty-two years. They concluded that "among the boys, the frequency of viewing television and liking violent programs at age eight were found to predict criminally antisocial behavior twenty-two years later."

Hattemer and Showers provide an overview of another study on the effects of TV violence conducted by Dr. Brandon Centerwall. From his research, Centerwall has concluded that heavy exposure to violent programming is causally related to roughly half of the twenty thousand murders each year in the United States. Data also indicates that violent TV content is causally related to half the rapes, assaults, and other forms of interpersonal violence in the United States. Centerwall published his conclusions in the June 1992 issue of *The Journal of the American Medical Association*.

Impressionable children and teens often imitate the actions they see on TV, in music, and in film. *Bringing out the Worst in Us: The Frightening Truth about Violence, the Media, and Our Youth*, published by Focus on the Family, clearly shows the connection between antisocial messages in the media and the negative effects they can have on children or teens. One story illustrates this truth: In March of 1995, Jason Edward Lewis grabbed his father's shotgun, loaded it with shells, and walked into the living room of his family's mobile home. Angry at being given an 11:00 p.m. curfew, the teen fired off numerous blasts and killed both of his parents. What was the inspiration for this violent killing spree? Police investigators said Jason had told his friends he wanted to live out the fantasy world of the serial killer depicted in Oliver Stone's film, *Natural Born Killers*. As it turned out, several of Jason's friends also wanted to go on a killing spree. They had all planned to run away from home and randomly kill people until they themselves were killed.

A more recent example of how "entertainment" can negatively influence children is the case of Richard Kuntz, a fifteen-year-old who had become fascinated with the CD *Antichrist Superstar* by the satanic rock star Marilyn Manson.

In 1996 Richard approached his father to tell him he had a new CD. His father told him he didn't want that kind of music in his home, but he never followed up to make sure the CD was thrown away. Two weeks later his wife, Christine, found Richard dead in his bedroom. The CD was on the stereo. The lyrics in Manson's song "The Reflecting God" encourage listeners to kill themselves. Richard had complied.

Appendix 2: The Homosexual Agenda

We shall sodomize your sons, emblems of your feeble masculinity, of your shallow dreams and vulgar lies. . . . Your sons shall become our minions and do our bidding. They will be recast in our image. They will come to crave and adore us. . . .

All churches who condemn us will be closed. Our holy gods are handsome young men. We adhere to a cult of beauty, moral and esthetics. All that is ugly and vulgar and banal will be annihilated. Since we are alienated from middle-class heterosexual conventions, we are free to live our lives according to the dictates of the pure imagination. For us, too much is not enough.

—*Michael Swift, Gay Revolutionary*

Michael Swift's warning to Christians and to the heterosexual world were printed in the February 15, 1987, issue of the *Boston Gay Community News* and later reprinted in an issue of the *American Family Association Journal*. Swift's views are not his alone. They belong to hundreds of thousands of homosexuals who are part of the gay rights movement.

Most Americans are ignorant about the objectives of the gay rights movement for two reasons. First, the mainstream media has been very careful to prevent Americans from getting a clear understanding of what "gay rights" is all about. Second, most Christians don't want to defile themselves by reading about aberrant sexual behaviors in publications targeted to gay-only audiences. Homosexuals are brutally honest about their goals and their sexual behaviors in their publications, yet few "straights" take the time to read these magazines or newspapers.

This ignorance among Christians can be destructive, not only to the culture at large, but to religious freedom as well. Christian attorney Roger Magnuson has addressed this problem in his book, *Informed Answers to Gay Rights Questions:*

"Although there is a natural and wholesome reluctance on the part of decent people to explore the details of deviant behavior, that reluctance must be tempered by a need to give society a commonsense understanding about the nature and public costs of perverted sexual behavior . . . society needs to know which kind of behavior it is being asked to accept as socially legitimate."

Gays, says Magnuson, have used certain terms to intimidate the opposition into silence.

"The homosexuals' use of clever expressions to convey a hidden meaning has been well explored by various writers. To be 'compassionate' means to accept homosexual behavior. A 'stable, loving relationship' means that homosexual pairings are equivalent to marriage. 'Stereotyping' means it is irrational to assume that all homosexual practices are wrong. 'Sexual minority' suggests that homosexuals are a legitimate minority. All such expressions are designed to put nonhomosexuals on the defensive."

Magnuson also points out that a gay rights law passed in Duluth, Minnesota, but eventually overturned by a vote of the people, was so broadly written that it would have allowed a homosexual male to come to work in drag and the employer could not have protested. If he had objected, he would have been guilty of causing mental anguish to the cross-dresser.

A CHRISTIAN'S BIBLICAL RESPONSE

In the New Testament the clearest exposition of God's opposition to homosexuality as a sinful behavior is found in Romans 1:24–28. In the verses leading up to verse 24, Paul described a person who has rejected God in his mind and whose thinking about the things of God has become futile.

What is the result of this rebellion? Verses 24–28 say: "Therefore God gave them over in the sinful desires of their hearts to sexual impurity for the degrading of their bodies with one another. They exchanged the truth of God for a lie, and worshiped and served created things rather than the Creator—who is forever praised. Amen. Because of this, God gave them over to shameful lusts. Even their women exchanged natural relations for unnatural ones. In the same way the men also abandoned natural relations with women and were inflamed with lust for one another. Men committed indecent acts with other men, and received in themselves the due penalty for their perversions. Furthermore, since they did not think it worthwhile to retain the knowledge of God, he gave them over to a depraved mind."

This section of Scripture is unmistakable in its condemnation of homosexual behavior. The Old Testament is even more explicit in condemning homosexual acts. In Leviticus 18:22 we read, "Do not lie with a man as one lies with a woman; that is detestable." Leviticus 20:13 states: "If a man lies with a man as one lies with a woman, both of them have done what is detestable. They must be put to death; their blood will be on their own heads." Throughout the Bible various words are used to describe homosexual conduct: *an abomination, lust, wicked, vile affections, against nature, unseemly, strange flesh,* and even *dogs* (referring to homosexual prostitutes in Deut. 23:18, KJV). The destruction of Sodom and Gomorrah by fire and brimstone is a compelling example of how the Lord feels about homosexual conduct.

The AIDS Tragedy

By focusing on homosexuality as a civil rights issue, the media conveniently ignores the reality of homosexual behavior as the cause of the spread of AIDS. More than 340,000 Americans have already died of AIDS. More than 550,000 are infected. A new infection occurs every eight and a half minutes.

In late November 1997 the United Nations announced that new estimates of HIV infection worldwide are one-third higher than originally thought.

• More than thirty million people worldwide have the AIDS virus.

• Sixteen thousand people are infected every day.

• One in every one hundred sexually active adults worldwide is infected with HIV.

• Only one in ten knows they are infected.

• At the current rate, more than forty million will be infected by 2000.

• An estimated 2.3 million people died of AIDS in 1997, a 50 percent increase over 1996. Nearly half of those deaths were women; 460,000 were children under fifteen.

THE DEADLY TRUTH

Homosexual conduct is dangerous both to the mental and physical health of gays and lesbians. It is unhealthy not only because of the danger of HIV infection; it is unhealthy because of the number of other sexually transmitted diseases (STDs) potentially contracted during sexual contact.

Dr. Jeffrey Satinover is a psychoanalyst and psychiatrist who has worked with homosexuals struggling with sexual identity disorders. He is a Christian and a medical advisor to Focus on the Family. In his recently published book *Homosexuality and the Politics of Truth* (Baker Book House), Satinover describes a typical homosexual as one who has:

• A twenty-five- to thirty-year decrease in life expectancy.

• Chronic, potentially fatal, liver disease—infectious hepatitis—which increases the risk of liver cancer.

- A much higher than usual incidence of suicide.
- Multiple bowel and other infectious diseases.
- Inevitably fatal immune disease including associated cancers.

A survey indicated that 78 percent of homosexuals have been infected at least once by an STD and that large numbers of them have been infected with herpes, venereal warts, and intestinal parasites. Homosexuals have a rate of infectious hepatitis B that is twenty to fifty times higher than the general populace. In San Francisco during the first decade liberal gay rights laws went into effect, the city saw an increase in the venereal disease rate twenty-two times the national average. Venereal disease clinics treated seventy-five thousand people every year during that decade, and 80 percent were homosexuals.

While Michael Eisner and The Walt Disney Company believe they are simply "affirming an alternate lifestyle," they are actually promoting the death of countless men and women who will die of HIV-related diseases.

WHO IS TRULY COMPASSIONATE?

A father and mother whose son was addicted to cocaine would not be considered compassionate if they "affirmed" their son's addiction and helped supply him with more cocaine or better ways of injecting the drug into his veins. The wife whose husband is a violent alcoholic is not showing him compassion by allowing him to beat her or watching in silence as he drinks himself to death. We do not affirm such destructive behaviors. Nor should we as a society or as individuals affirm a lifestyle that has led to hundreds of thousands of deaths over the past decade. In addition, we should not be giving our money to organizations that are promoting a behavior that kills people.

The truly compassionate response is to actively oppose the gay rights movement and to do whatever we can to help homosexuals overcome their life-controlling sexual addictions. We should affirm those things that bring life and freedom; we should vigorously oppose those behaviors that bring bondage and death to others.

Appendix 3: The Resolution

THE SOUTHERN BAPTIST CONVENTION BOYCOTT RESOLUTION

This Resolution was passed at the 1997 Southern Baptist Convention and followed the passage of an earlier resolution to monitor The Disney Company's products in 1996. Resolutions are not authoritative and are not binding, but they are instructive as a guide to where the majority of Southern Baptists stand with respect to particular issues at the particular time in history when the resolution was passed.

1997 SBC RESOLUTION ON MORAL STEWARDSHIP AND THE DISNEY COMPANY

WHEREAS, Everything Christians possess of time, money, and resources is given to them by God as a stewardship for which they will give an account before a holy God; and

WHEREAS, Those who serve the public in any manner also have a stewardship before God regarding their service, and those who have greater influence have greater responsibility for their stewardship and must give a greater accounting; and

WHEREAS, Many entertainment providers including, but not limited to, The Disney Company are increasingly promoting immoral ideologies such as homosexuality, infidelity, and adultery, which are biblically reprehensible and abhorrent to God and His plan for the world that He loves; and

WHEREAS, The 1996 Southern Baptist Convention passed a resolution regarding these issues with a specific appeal to The Disney Company, which had long been a respected leader of family entertainment in keeping with traditional moral values; and

WHEREAS, The aforementioned resolution called for our Christian Life Commission to monitor Disney's progress in returning to its previous philosophy of producing enriching family entertainment; and the Christian Life Commission has now reported that The Disney Company has not only ignored our concerns, but flagrantly furthered this moral digression in its product and policies; and

WHEREAS, We realize that we cannot do everything to stop the moral decline in our nation, but we must do what lies before us when it is right through a proper use of our influence, energies, and prayers, particularly when it affects our nation's children;

BE IT THEREFORE RESOLVED, That the messengers of the Southern Baptist Convention meeting in Dallas, Texas, June 17-19, 1997, urge every Southern Baptist to take the stewardship of their time, money, and resources so seriously that they refrain from patronizing The Disney Company and any of its related entities, understanding that this is not an attempt to bring The Disney Company down, but to bring Southern Baptists up to the moral standard of God; and

BE IT FURTHER RESOLVED, That we encourage Southern Baptists to refrain from patronizing any company that promotes immoral ideologies and practices, realizing that The Disney Company is not the only such provider; and

BE IT FURTHER RESOLVED, That we ask our pastors and church leaders to become informed regarding these issues and teach their people accordingly, and that we urge all Southern Baptists to graciously communicate the reasons for their individual actions to The Disney Company and other companies; and

BE IT FINALLY RESOLVED, That we pray that God would use these actions to help the employees of such companies to respect the enormous stewardship they have before God, and we affirm those employees who embrace and share our concerns.

Appendix 4: Mickey's Family Tree

The Walt Disney Company is one of the largest media and entertainment companies in the world and is, for all practical purposes, two companies in one with the acquisition of Capital Cities/ABC.

The following information traces the ownership of various enterprises that reportedly answer to The Disney Company through various divisions and subsidiaries of Disney and ABC/Capital Cities.[*]

FILM, TELEVISION, AND MUSIC: DISNEY OWNED

Walt Disney Pictures
Touchstone Pictures
Hollywood Pictures
Caravan Pictures
Miramax Films

*List of Disney holdings as of 1996.

Film distribution rights for independent production companies
Cinergi Pictures Entertainment
Interscope Communications and Merchant-Ivory Productions
Walt Disney Home Video
Buena Vista Television
Touchstone Television
Walt Disney Television
The Disney Channel
Walt Disney Theatrical Productions
Hollywood Records
Wonderland Music
Walt Disney Music Company
Lyric Street Records

CAPITAL CITIES/ABC OWNED

ABC Television Network
ABC News
ABC Sports
ABC Radio Network
ESPN
Lifetime (jointly owned with Hearst)
A&E Network (jointly owned with Hearst and NBC)
WASC-AM, New York, NY
KABC-AM, Los Angeles, CA
KMPC-AM, Los Angeles, CA
WLS-AM, Chicago, IL
KGO -AM, San Francisco, CA
WJR -AM, Detroit, MI
WBAP -AM, Arlington, TX
WMAL-AM, Washington, D.C.
WKHX -AM, Atlanta, GA
KQRS -AM, Minneapolis-St. Paul, MN
WPLJ-FM, New York, NY
KLOS-FM, Los Angeles, CA

WLS-FM, Chicago, IL
WHYT-FM, Detroit, Ml
KSCS-FM, Arlington, TX
WRQX-FM, Washington, D.C.
WABC-TV, New York, NY
KABC-TV, Los Angeles, CA
WLS-TV, Chicago, IL
WPVI-TV, Philadelphia, PA
KGO-TV, San Francisco, CA
KTRK-TV, Houston, TX
WTVD-TV, Raleigh-Durham, NC
KFSN-TV, Fresno, CA

THEME PARKS AND RESORTS: DISNEY OWNED

Walt Disney World, Orlando, FL (consists of 3 theme parks, 12 resort hotels, RV/camping park, 5 golf courses, 3 water parks);
Disneyland, Anaheim, CA (theme park and 1,100-room hotel)
Tokyo Disneyland, Tokyo, Japan
Euro-Disney, Paris, France

VACATION PLANNING AND PROVIDER SERVICES: DISNEY OWNED

Disney Vacation Club-Orlando, FL
Disney Vacation Club-Vero Beach, FL
Disney Vacation Club-Hilton Head Island, SC
Disney Coronado Springs Resort
Disney Cruise Lines
Walt Disney Travel

MANAGEMENT AND DESIGN SERVICES: DISNEY OWNED

Walt Disney Imagineering
Disney Development Company

REAL ESTATE: DISNEY OWNED

Celebration Florida, a planned community designed and developed by Disney

PUBLISHING: DISNEY OWNED

Mouse Works Publishing
Disney Press
Hyperion Press
Hyperion Press for Kids
Disney Hachette Editions
Disney Adventures magazine
Discover magazine
FamilyFun magazine
Family PC magazine

PUBLICATIONS: CAPITAL CITIES/ABC OWNED

TRADE JOURNALS

Children's Business
Daily News Record
Footwear News
Home Furnishings Daily
Home Fashions
SportsStyle
Supermarket News
Women's Wear Daily
American Metal Market
Assembly
Automotive Body Repair News
Automotive Industries
Automotive Marketing

CED

Cablevision
Commercial Carrier Journal
Convergence
Distribution
Electronic Industry Telephone
Directory
Energy User News
Expansion
Feedstuffs
Food Engineering
Food Engineering International
Food Formulating
Food Master
Hardware Age
HazMat Shipping
Industrial Maintenance & Plant
Operation
Industrial Paint & Powder
Industrial Safety & Hygiene
Jewelers Circular-Keystone
Manufacturing Systems
Metal Center News
Motor Age
Multichannel News
New Steel
Obras
Owner Operator
Product Design and development
Quality Review
Tacks 'n Togs Merchandising
Selling
Software Solutions
Video Business

Video Software Magazine
Warehousing Management
Wireless Week

MEDICAL JOURNALS
Review of Ophthalmology
Review of Optometry
Clinical Psychiatry News
Family Practice News
Internal Medicine News
Ob.Gyn News
Pediatric News
Skin and Allergy News

GENERAL INTEREST AND ADVERTISING NEWSPAPERS: CAPITAL CITIES/ABC OWNED
The Advertiser, Branford, CT
Abington-Rockland Mariner, Rockland, MA
Albany Democrat-Herald, Albany, OR
Armada Times, Armada, MI
Braintree Forum, Braintree, MA
Branford Review, Branford, CT
Brown City Banner, Brown City, MI
Canton News, Canton, CT
Clinton Recorder, Clinton, CT
Cohassett Mariner, Cohassett, MA
Cottage Grove Sentinel, Cottage Grove, OR
Daily Tidings, Ashland, OR
Gresham Outlook, Gresham, OR
The Oakland Press, Pontiac, MI
Hamden Chronicle, Hamden, CT
Hanover Mariner, Hanover, MA
Highland News-Leader, Highland, IL
Hingham Mariner, Hingham, MA
Holbrook Sun, Holbrook, MA

Kingston Independent Voice, Kingston, MA
Lebanon Express, Lebanon, OR
Little Nickel Want Ads, Lynnwood, WA
Marshfield Mariner, Marshfield, MA
Milford Citizen, Milford, CT
Narragansett Times, Wakefield, RI
Newport News-Times, Newport, OR
Niantic News, Niantic, CT
Nickel Ads, Portland, OR
Nickel Nik, Spokane, WA
Norwell Mariner, Norwell, MA
O'Fallon Progress, O'Fallon, IL
Pembroke Mariner, Pembroke, MA
The Pendulum, East Greenwich, CT
Cape Cod Pennysaver, Cape Cod, MA
Pictorial Gazette, Old Lyme, CT
Prairie Farmer, Lombard, IL
Randolph Mariner, Randolph, MA
Regional Standard, Colchester, CT
Sandy Post, Sandy, OR
Scituate Mariner, Scituate, MA
Shore Line Times, Guilford, CT
Springfield News, Springfield, OR
Standard Times, North Kingstown, RI
St. Louis Countian, Clayton, MO
St. Louis Daily Record, St, Louis, MO
Weymouth News, Weymouth, MA
Sparta News-Plaindealer, Sparta, IL

MAGAZINES

Los Angeles Magazine
Institutional Investor

PUBLISHING COMPANIES

Diversified Publishing Group

Fairchild Publications
Financial Services Publishing Group
Agricultural Publishing Group
Chilton Enterprises
Farm Progress Publications
Imprint, Inc.
NILS Publishing Company
Chilton Book Company
Chilton Datalog
Miller Publishing Company
Hitchcock Publishing Company
Wilson Publishing Company

RETAIL DISNEY OWNED

The Disney Store
UNOCO

EDUCATIONAL PRODUCTS DISNEY OWNED

Childcraft Education
Corporation
Disney Educational Productions

PROFESSIONAL SPORTS FRANCHISES DISNEY OWNED

The Mighty Ducks of Anaheim (Professional Hockey Team)
The Anaheim Angels Baseball Club

MISCELLANEOUS ENTERPRISES DISNEY OWNED

Reedy Creek Energy Services
Vista Insurance Services
WCO Port Properties

CAPITAL CITIES/ABC OWNED

Chilton Research Services
Chilton Management Information Systems
Chilton Direct Marketing & List Management Company
Professional Exposition Management Company
Legal-Communications Corp.

The companies on this list were compiled from documents filed with the Securities and Exchange Commission by Disney and Capital Cities/ABC and from the 1995 edition of the Directory of Corporate Affiliations.

This list is provided as a public service only. We are unable to vouch for the complete accuracy of the list as some corporations may have been sold or otherwise liquidated out of the Disney Company portfolio. See www.erlc.com for an updated list.

Appendix 5: Why A Radio Program?

Dr. Richard Land

Why add another radio talk show to the nation's airwaves? The answer lies in the kind of talk show that "For Faith & Family" has become. For several years now the Ethics & Religious Liberty Commission's trustees and staff have been impressed that God was leading the ERLC toward a national radio ministry in order to spread the message of Christians being the salt and the light Christ commanded them to be.

In fact, in recent years people kept asking us, "When are you going to be on radio?" "Why can't we have a program that deals with the cutting-edge moral and spiritual issues we face as a nation?"

"For Faith & Family" is both the ERLC's response to the deeply felt providential leadership of the Holy Spirit and our answer to the throngs of people who have expressed their desire for a live, interactive radio program where they can ask about the issues in today's headlines, not last week's or last month's news.

"For Faith & Family's" mission is to proclaim the changeless truths of the Bible and to apply them to the ever-changing issues of the world. Each day my guests and I will each seek to lift up the divine truth of Scripture and to explain God's changeless standards in everyday language to the listening audience.

We believe upholding and preaching God's standard of truth and right and wrong is an essential and necessary part of the evangelist's task. "For Faith & Family" will seek to proclaim "the faith" of the Gospel of Jesus as revealed in Holy Scripture and to apply its timeless truths to the issues impacting you and your family on a daily basis.

Each day "For Faith & Family" will lead with an issue from the day's news and then will seek to apply the truths of Scripture to that issue to help us to think "Christianly" about it. That way, on an issue-by-issue, example-by-example, case-by-case basis we will together seek to construct a Christian mind, perspective, and outlook on the challenging and unprecedented moral and spiritual questions of the day.

New and critical issues continue to challenge our beliefs and threaten our families in the months and years ahead. "For Faith & Family" promises to tackle these issues from a biblical perspective head on, no matter how controversial, and to do so without compromise.

The Bible itself tells us that "the whole creation groaneth and travaileth in pain together until now" waiting for "the redemption" (Rom. 8:22-23, KJV). Everything and everyone has been warped and distorted and cursed by sin and the fall. Nothing in this world is as God intended it to be, except for one thing—the Bible. God's Holy Word is the only tangible thing in the entire world that is exactly as God intended it to be and is utterly uncorrupted by sin.

That is why James describes the Word of God as being like a divine "mirror," the only place where we can see the "true" truth, undistorted and clear, about ourselves as well as the world:

> Anyone who listens to the word but does not do what it says is like a man who looks at his face in a mirror and, after looking at himself, goes away and immediately forgets what he looks like. But the man who looks intently into the perfect law that gives freedom, and continues to do this, not forgetting what he has heard, but doing it—he will be blessed in what he does. (Jas. 1:23-25, NIV)

"For Faith & Family" seeks, with God's help, to hold up the perfect "mirror" of God's Word and help each of us to see what needs to be seen, and then changed and adjusted in accordance with His Word. Then we will truly be equipped to be the salt and the light Jesus commanded us to be (Matt. 5:13-16).

The ERLC launched its thirty minute, live, interactive call-in radio program across the nation on Monday, February 16, 1998. "For Faith & Family" airs live from 11:30 a.m. to 12:00 noon Central Time Monday through Friday each week and is available either live or through tape delay on as many as 180 stations in 33 states. The program is also available live on the Internet at Light-Source on AudioNet anywhere in North America and throughout most of the world. **(Visit www.erlc.com for additional information, or call the ERLC at 1-615-244-2495.)**

I hope and pray you will listen and call us with your questions and comments at 1-888-FAITH-56. Thanks for listening. God bless you, your family, and God bless America.

For Further Reading

ON THE GAY RIGHTS AGENDA, MINISTRY, AND THE POWER OF THE MEDIA

You can order these titles from Christian and secular bookstores as well as from Amazon Books on the Internet. If you have not yet learned to use the Internet, we would urge that you do. It is an excellent way of staying informed on the gay rights movement, the Disney boycott, and other events that affect your life and the life of your family.

After the Ball: How America Will Conquer Its Fear and Hatred of Gays in the 90s—Marshall Kirk and Hunter Madsen. This book, written by two gay strategists, clearly outlines a publicity campaign to normalize homosexuality and to vilify the opposition to homosexual conduct. This campaign strategy is being implemented at all levels of society, within schools, and through the media. Published by Plume Books, a division of Penguin.

And That's the Way It Isn't: A Reference Guide to Media Bias—This book is published by the Media Research Center (MRC), a conservative media-watchdog group based in Virginia. This fact-packed volume provides the reader with a number of studies of media and Hollywood elites showing that they are typically liberal, anti-Christian, and tolerant of infidelity and homosexuality. MRC also has a Web site.

Bringing out the Worst in Us: The Frightening Truth about Violence, the Media, and Our Youth—Bob Waliszewski and Jerry Melchisedeck. This well-researched book carefully documents how sex and violence in music, the Internet, video games, films, and TV affect our youth. Published by Focus on the Family, Youth Culture Department.

Coming Out of Homosexuality—Bob Davies and Lori Rentzel. Davies is executive director of Exodus International, one of the most effective counseling ministries to homosexuals in the U.S. *Coming Out* describes homosexual struggles and what a person must do to become spiritually whole and free from sexual bondage. Published by Intervarsity Press.

Disney and the Bible—Perucci Ferraiuolo. The author takes a historical look at The Disney Company and details the company's promotion of homosexuality, sexual promiscuity, occultism, anti-Christian messages, and more.

Don't Touch That Dial: The Impact of the Media on Children and the Family—Barbara Hattemer and Robert Showers. The authors are experts on the effects of pornography and violence in our culture. This book explains the power of the media and the effect pornographic and violent images have on adults and children. Published by Huntington House Publishers.

Informed Answers to Gay Rights Questions—Roger Magnuson. The author is a lawyer and ordained preacher who has written extensively on the gay rights movement from a moral and legal standpoint. Magnuson debunks many of the gay myths in this book. Published by Multnomah.

Hollywood vs. America—Michael Medved. The author, a film critic for PBS, is also an orthodox Jew who has written extensively in defense of pro-Christian messages in the entertainment industry. Medved's 386-page book is a treasure of insights into how Hollywood producers think and how their antireligious ideas are promoted through film and TV. Published by HarperPerennial Books.

Homosexuality: A Freedom Too Far—Dr. Charles Socarides, a well-respected psychiatrist associated with NARTH. Socarides has opposed the normalization of homosexuality within the medical community for decades. This book is written in a question-and-answer format for easy access to troubling questions about homosexuality. Published by Adam Margrave Books.

Homosexuality and the Politics of Truth—Dr. Jeffrey Satinover is also a respected psychiatrist and currently serves as a medical advisor to Focus on the Family. Satinover's book debunks faulty gay science and points out the serious medical problems caused by homosexual conduct. He also deals with sexual orientation from a medical viewpoint.

Kingdoms in Conflict: An Insider's Challenging View of Politics, Power, and the Pulpit—Chuck Colson, founder of Prison Fellowship, explains how the Christian is actually a citizen of two worlds: the culture he lives in and the kingdom of God. Colson describes how Christians can live for God in a hostile culture. Published by Morrow/Zondervan.

The Other Side of Tolerance: Victims of Homosexual Activism—Published by the Family Research Council, Washington, D.C. This book describes thirty-two cases of violence or intimidation against businessmen, pastors, hospice workers, and more who oppose the gay rights movement.

What Is Secular Humanism? Why Humanism Became Secular and How It Is Changing Our World—Dr. James Hitchcock. The author's chapter on the power of the mass media is worth the price of this book. In it he describes how anti-Christian forces, led by Norman Lear, took control of the media in the 1960s and began introducing a new secular morality into popular culture. Published by Servant Books.

Dr. Richard D. Land is President and Chief Executive Officer of the Ethics and Religious Liberty Commission, the Southern Baptist Convention's agency for "applied Christianity." Prior to becoming the Ethics and Religious Liberty Commission's president, Dr. Land served as The Criswell College's Vice-President for Academic Affairs from 1980 to 1988. While on leave of absence from The Criswell College, Dr. Land served from January 1987 to May 1988 as Administrative Assistant to the Honorable William P. Clements, Jr., Governor of Texas. Dr. Land was the Governor's senior advisor on church-state issues and areas relating to "traditional family values" as well as antidrug, antipornography, and antiabortion legislation.

Dr. Land graduated from Princeton University (B.A.; magna cum laude), Oxford University (D.Phil.), and New Orleans Baptist Theological Seminary (M.Div.).

Frank York is a freelance writer. He is former editor and writer in the Public Policy Department at Focus on the Family, where he served for eight years. He began his professional writing career in 1980 at the Christian Broadcasting Network as a writer/researcher for a film documentary on pornography. Later he served as staff writer for Tim and Beverly LaHaye in Washington, D.C. In 1993 he authored *When the Wicked Seize a City*, a book describing the persecution of Pastor Chuck and Donna McIlhenny by gay rights activists in San Francisco.